# Expressions in Wood

J. Christopher White

*Companion Press*
**P.O. Box 351**
**Shippensburg, PA 17257**


ISBN 1-56043-430-9


For Worldwide Distribution
Printed in the U.S.A.

Photographs in this book were taken by the following photographers:
    George Dillman
    Jim Koschmann
    Mac Powers
    Cecil Simpson
    J. Christopher White
    James R. Rill, cover

# Contents

*This book is dedicated to Jesus Christ of Nazareth, God come in the flesh, without whose grace and talents no work in this book could have come to pass.*

# PREFACE

The arts, a means of expressing tender emotions—life's thoughts and moments illustrated and preserved in colors, earth and word. Art, a voice amplified by melodies and harmonies springing from an open heart in an attempt to share a beauty, a truth or a concern. What is the mystique of art, the deep rooted attraction? Is it the reminder of a deeper realm in which we share our existence, a world that escapes the violence of storms and waves in the rushing air of the superficial? This deeper world responds to the crashing waves above in gentle, fluid sways and spins amid the filtered echos of the din above, speaking of an even deeper rest beyond its emerald air. Within each of us is a memory, a song, if you will, drawing our hearts back to a land through which we passed in childhood and on towards *something more.*

Art is an expression of the soul, a singing of the song. It is the soul—the mind, the emotions and the will—that passes beneath the rippled surface to view that gentle realm and then returns to relate a glimpse of her beauty.

There is a peace, a fulfillment, an answer to the yearnings of the heart, to the fears and questions of the soul. After years of painful dives into the shallow, rocky waters of religion and *self*-sufficiency, an exhausted swimmer gave up the struggle and cried for a helping hand. Finally he took the hand of the man who walked on water, made the sea, and accepted suffocation in the place of the swimmer. Not only did He draw me into the gentle, restful refuge of His love, but He gave me gifts—the greatest of which is eternal life—and the privilege and power to actually *know* and *love* the Lord Jesus Christ. His love has filled my heart, healed my wounds, and opened my eyes to the beauty of the world around me. He has allowed me to see Him in all His creation and, more importantly, to be immersed in the realization that I am forever His, precious and much loved. I pray and trust that His gentle, yet majestic hand may be seen reaching through the pages of this book, and that, through the gifts He has given me, I may express my love to Him by revealing His love to you.

As it takes an open heart to voice the melodies of the soul, so it takes an open heart to hear them.

# LAY BARE YOUR HEART

What happens as we grow older to the carefree and trusting attitude of a child? For some it ends bitterly at a young age; others still surely lose it a care at a time through the years, while a blessed few regain, not retain, a heart that functions according to its design.

In speaking of a burglary of her home, a friend recently told me, "They got little of value, save my confidence in human nature." From the circumstances she could see that the burglar had to be someone she knew. A stranger could not have stolen that confidence.

Those we love are the ones equipped to cut us the deepest, for we let them into the innermost parts of our hearts and seldom trust them enough to let them back in to repair the damage they cause through their almost certain failures. Wounds, self-inflicted through our own sins, are often the hardest to heal. They fester with guilt and condemnation, and lie guarded by shame and fear. Thus, we, to varying degrees, go through life pained, scarred and unable to freely give and receive the love God has for us.

Becoming a Christian does not instantly repair the damage inflicted by a life of sin in a cruel world, but it does open a channel so that we may come to know the Healer. Jesus Christ is a gentleman—He won't force His way into an aching heart; He waits until we open up in trust and allow Him to work. Sometimes that work includes the hands of one of His children. As we trust *Him in* others, our trust in others rebuilds.

*A lovely form hides a broken heart
    no more with childlike trust,
for a heart that beats in a fallen world
    must form a calloused crust,*

*that keeps out pain or any chance
    of being hurt again
but by guarding against enmity
    it also keeps out friends.*

*There are hands that formed this very heart
    while it beat within the womb,
and will seek to own this broken heart
    'til it lies still in the tomb.*

*So what proof is there that I can trust
    someone with such demands?
The proof is evidenced you see
    by the nail scars in His hands.*

*Not just His hands, but His heart as well,
    were pierced for you that day,
when He bore your sins, and in your place
    died to make a way,*

*to allow His love to enter,
    when you trust this risen Lord,
so His love could heal your wounds and scars
    your childhood heart restore.*

**Confess your faults one to another, and pray one for another, that ye may be healed.**
**The effectual fervent prayer of a righteous man availeth much.**
**James 5:16**

West Texas Juniper

Height 31″

# SECOND CHANCE

I guess this poem could conceivably go with any wood sculpture. This particular piece came from a beautiful old dead tree that was precariously perched on the sloping edge of a high cliff. Each year the tree had put on rings of different width depending on how much moisture it received. The drought years formed dark areas, the lush years golden bands. At an average growth rate of 1/64th of an inch a year, this tree widened into a substantial piece of wood.

One morning I got the idea to *go carve me a peacock* and clearly saw its form in the old tree. *Well, old tree, get ready for a change.* Eight hundred work hours and two hundred pounds of wood chips later, the transformation was complete. The tree could have ended up a splintered heap at the base of an obscure West Texas canyon wall, but in a sense it was redeemed.

A different aspect of the old tree's beauty can now be seen. Though still basically a tree, it's now a new creation.

**That which is born of the flesh is flesh; and that which is born of the Spirit is spirit. Marvel not that I said unto thee, Ye must be born again. John 3:6-7**

*This piece of wood records the times
    and trials of this fair land;
each time of poor or plenty
    is marked by a double band.*

*The many years together
    shape a pattern and a form.
The hand of God, through hand of man,
    gives this tree a life reborn.*

*By submitting to the will of God
    this twig became a timber,
in yielding up its ancient shape
    became a beauty to remember.*

*For one thing is most certain
    **all** control is in God's hand,
whether it be the shaping of a tree
    or His plan for the life of man.*

*So don't resist the Master's hand
    when He moves to shape your life;
a masterpiece He'll make you,
    unless you twist beneath the knife,*

*and cause by your own wisdom,
    the blindness to remain
when by trusting God and His loving Son,
    you could be born to live again.*

***Therefore if any man be in Christ, he is a new creature: old things are passed away;***
***behold, all things are become new.***
***II Corinthians 5:17***

West Texas Juniper on Walnut

Height 23″ Length 51″

# HE KNOWS WHERE TO HIDE

It is an impressive sight to see a blue quail glide the last twenty yards before banking sharply into the midst of a cactus patch. That is what I tried to portray in this sculpture. Since this plump little ground dweller is a prime choice on the menu of most every predator, the fact that they survive at all shows the truth of the title of this piece.

We as humans are in a battle. We really do have an enemy of our souls who seeks to destroy us. As if having a diabolical enemy were not bad enough, each of us also possesses a traitor in our ranks called the flesh or carnal mind. *"Because the carnal mind is enmity against God: for it is not subject to the law of God, neither indeed can be"* (Romans 8:7). In other words this traitor can never be trusted and will always let the enemy past the lines of our best defense.

We cannot hide from ourselves, so where do we flee for help? How do we escape a battle that follows us to our most secret refuge?

I wish I had room to share all of Psalms 91 with you. God's many promises in this song start with: *"He that dwelleth in the secret place of the most High shall abide under the shadow of the Almighty. I will say of the Lord, He is my refuge and my fortress: my God; in him will I trust"* (Psalms 91:1-2).

The shifting sands of situational ethics provide no firm footing in the storms of life nor do structures built upon them afford any lasting refuge. We have a God who is Almighty, Holy, always there and always the same. He provides peace in the midst of the storm, even during the storms that rage inside us. We have only to flee in faith to the One who has power over the storms. *"Thou wilt keep him in perfect peace, whose mind is stayed on thee; because he trusteth in thee"* (Isaiah 26:3). Do not take my word. Listen to the words of King David, a man hunted like an animal for several years: *"Trust in him at all times: ye people, pour out your heart before him: God is a refuge for us.* **Selah** [meaning, meditate on that]*"* (Psalms 62:8).

Psalms 62 and 91; Isaiah 26:3; John 14:27

*A pleasure to watch*
  *a quail glide in flight,*
*as he ducks down in hiding*
  *'neath the thorns for the night.*

*Knowing the place*
  *that is safest to hide,*
*trusting he'll rest*
  *if in there he'll abide.*

*In the battle of life*
  *we're no match for the fight*
*and our pride often hinders*
  *both the fight and the flight.*

*And we fall by not trusting*
  *the almighty Lord;*
*we waste His provisions*
  *of shield and of sword.*

*When in trusting as children*
  *we turn fearful eyes*
*to an almighty God*
  *we're set free from the lies,*

*that torment and hinder*
  *and rob us of peace;*
*in obedient trust*
  *we at last find release.*

*Because he hath set his love upon me, therefore will I deliver him: I will set him on high,*
*because he hath known my name. He shall call upon me and I will answer him:*
*I will be with him in trouble; I will deliver him, and honour him.*
**Psalms 91:14-15**

West Texas Juniper and Black Mesquite on Walnut Base

Height 17″

# THE SMALL AND THE GREAT

There are always two sides of the trail off which to stray. The folly of comparing ourselves to others is a subject that never ceases to amaze me (it must, because I do it so often). When you think about it, what other exercise has such instant and painful results. We turn on the tube and see a perfect smile being joyously brushed with some substance that will make our teeth as alluring as those flashing across the screen. *Yeah right, maybe with braces and a can of white spray paint, but then there is always the rest of the face.* I will not go on about the flawless physiques dancing in the suds, or the elegant homes and cars they dash about in. I believe my point is made. I think we all can see the folly of stepping off that side of the path. The other side of the trail is a step into pride and put down that, in the long run, is equally painful, though more evident to others than ourselves.

Gaining self-worth from the gifts God gives us, whether physical beauty, talents or possessions, is an exercise in futility. There is no guarantee we will keep any of them, and someone will always have more or better. There is within us a need to be valued and accepted for simply who we are. True self-worth comes from knowing that someone accepts you and values you because "you are you." How wonderful if that person happens to be the Person who made all those people we have been comparing ourselves to. How much greater the wonder to realize He values you enough to have died for you. How awe inspiring to realize that He will conform you to His image if you will let Him.

Romans 5:6     II Corinthians 3:18

*Swimming there beneath the sea*
*he wonders what he's meant to be;*
*"for I'm so small and others great,*
*at times it hurts so much to wait."*

*He dreams someday of open seas,*
*of grandeur and of majesty;*
*"but I'm so small and others great,*
*I cannot seem to bear to wait."*

*"How shall I grow and be as them?"*
*he muses as he daily swims,*
*"for I'm so small and they're so great,*
*I'm sure they didn't have to wait."*

*This little fish is so unwise*
*he needs to see through other eyes,*
*and not compare the small and great*
*to miss the treasures in "the wait."*

*For as he swims he grows each day;*
*the swimming is the Maker's way*
*to slowly change the small to great.*
*You see, there really is no wait.*

*For we dare not make ourselves of the number, or compare ourselves with some
that commend themselves: but they measuring themselves by themselves,
and comparing themselves among themselves, are not wise.*
**II Corinthians 10:12**

West Texas Juniper and Black Mesquite

Height 14″

# MORE THAN A DOVE OR FLAME

A newborn babe cries out for food, and a loving parent gently responds. My spirit cried out for nourishment, and the Lord fed me on the milk of His Word. *Bible reading, alright, let's see now. I'll have a little Psalms today and another helping of Proverbs, some gospel and hey, what's this? Acts, looks like some good stuff. What on earth are you talking about here, Lord? You mean to tell me the Holy Spirit's a He and not an it? He's a real person, just like You and the Father? You mean He's here too? Uh, hi Holy Spirit . . . uh, sorry about that Chief . . . uh, what's that? . . . no, You aren't a little bitty dove are You?* Maybe it's because I didn't have many preconceived notions to dispel, but I soon found the Holy Spirit to be the most winsome member of the Trinity. *Hey Jesus, it was Him all along wasn't it? I knew Somebody was showing me all this good stuff here in the Bible.* My initial reaction was typical of one who doesn't understand God's infinite patience and mercy. *Hey, this is great. Now when Jesus and the Father are put out with me I'll just hang around the Holy Spirit.* Well, it doesn't really work that way, but it sure helps to realize that the Holy Spirit is a person, and He has a specific job to do in our lives. He does it quite well if we don't quench Him with our own fear, understanding and unbelief.

This prayer came out of that realization.

***But the Comforter, which is the Holy Ghost, whom the Father will send in my name, he shall teach you all things, and bring all things to your remembrance, whatsoever I have said unto you.* John 14:26**

*O Holy Spirit,
    this child of God does pray,
You light upon my aching heart
    and comfort me today.*

*And lo I find You're not a dove,
    an energy or flame,
but a happy, Godly person
    sent in Jesus' name.*

*Sent to show me where I am
    as I travel on this earth
to the Father and His loving Son
    in the land of my new birth.*

*An ambush waits at every turn
    should I ever stray my eyes,
from the Word of God, my Holy Guide,
    and look to worldly lies.*

*Your arms are full of weapons
    You give me to discern
the where abouts of satan
    as he waits for me to turn,*

*and gifts that I can praise You with
    the Father and the Son;
for this I thank the Lord, my God,
    and pray "Thy will be done."*

*Now there are diversities of gifts, but the same Spirit. And there are differences of administrations, but the same Lord. And there are diversities of operations, but it is the same God which worketh all in all. But the manifestation of the Spirit is given to every man to profit withal.*
**I Corinthians 12:4-7**

West Texas Juniper

Wingspan 16″

# CALLOUS PAIN

My hands are heavily calloused by reason of use. While working in Central Mexico, my heart, through exposure to the poverty, pain and hopelessness I saw daily in the faces of the people, began its own protective build-up, until one day I noticed I no longer *cared*. This realization brought pain and a desire to change. But how could I go about making myself care again? How could I cause true compassion to bloom in a garden of apathy, selfishness and self-pity?

Circumstances, pain and life in general can harden a heart into a cold, dark rock; only God can do anything to reverse this trend. How does God replace stone with flesh? Put simply, we have to trust Him with our *whole* heart, by giving Him our *broken* heart.

How did Jesus answer my prayers and cause me to let go of my foolish efforts to change? He revealed Himself through a ragged shepherd boy on the edge of a desolate Mexican canyon wall. As the boy and his flock made their way up from watering in the canyon floor, I noticed that the motionless wool draped around his shoulders was a day-old lamb. When I asked if the lamb was sick, he answered with a simple tenderness, "No, she was born out here today and was unable to make the climb up; so I'm carrying her." What the boy thought as I teared up and turned away did not bother me. I had seen such a picture of the sweetness and faithfulness of my Shepherd that I had to leave. More tears came as I was reminded of the times He had carried me through trials I could not bear. I began to desire, for His sake, that He love the hurting through me, for He truly aches for all His lambs. I made this piece to symbolize how God has taken the callouses off my heart, enabling me to care again.

*Spirit of the Living God take away my pain,*
*with all the gentleness You have make me feel again.*


*For I have lost the eyes that see within an aching heart,*
*and calloused over has become in me that selfsame part.*


*Rich in blessings, peace and joy given from above,*
*yet only as a channel can I comprehend Your love.*


- - - - - - -


*My child with all the strength of ten you couldn't budge the stone*
*for I've reserved all work as such for My very own.*


*So lift your eyes above you, in trust let go your hands;*
*a heart of flesh, through grace I'll give, just follow My commands.*

*A new heart also will I give you, and a new spirit will I put within you; and I will take away the stony heart out of your flesh, and I will give you an heart of flesh. And I will put my spirit within you, and cause you to walk in my statutes, and ye shall keep my judgments, and do them. And ye shall dwell in the land that I gave to your fathers; and ye shall be my people, and I will be your God.*
**Ezekiel 36:26-28**

West Texas Juniper

Height 10″

13

# WINGS OF PRAYER

Prayer is talking to and listening to God, your loving Maker. After the communication lines once downed by sin are reestablished through faith in Jesus, I wonder if we even begin to realize what we really possess in the privilege of prayer? Or are we like the curious roadrunner, who seems only to use his wings when all else fails? Does this sound familiar?

I heard the story of a preacher who asked a small boy if he prayed every day. The child responded, "Well no, some days I don't need anything." Does that remind you of anyone you know?

Okay then, if prayer is designed to be something more than petitioning and thanking God, then what exactly is it for? Have you ever wondered just who God is or exactly what Jesus thinks about you or feels toward you? God's word says that He so loved us He gave His only begotten Son, and through Him we have eternal life. But just as a love letter holds a certain assurance in it, there is still the need to hear "You're my heart's desire" from the one you love.

A healthy, intimate relationship is born and lives through the expression of one's love and commitment to the other—the opening up and sharing of one's heart with another. Trust grows in this garden and rest from striving to please. If we truly could realize what God our Father thinks of us and what we mean to Him, we would spend less time *persuading* Him to move on our behalf; and thus, we would have more time to focus on Him and appreciate Him for Who He is.

*The roadrunner*
  *so has his name,*
*For all folks know*
  *he runs his game.*

*His speedy gait*
  *seems to be*
*Sufficient when*
  *he's forced to flee.*

*So seldom seen*
  *and rarely heard*
*Are the flapping wings*
  *of this earthbound bird.*

*But come the times*
  *when feet do fail,*
*He glides on outstretched*
  *wings and tail.*

*Are we like him*
  *in our prayer,*
*We seldom come*
  *without some care*

*And call to God*
  *in frantic bursts*
*For our own wisdom*
  *we've tried first?*

*But if we'd pray*
  *to know our King*
*We'd glide aloft*
  *on eagle's wing.*

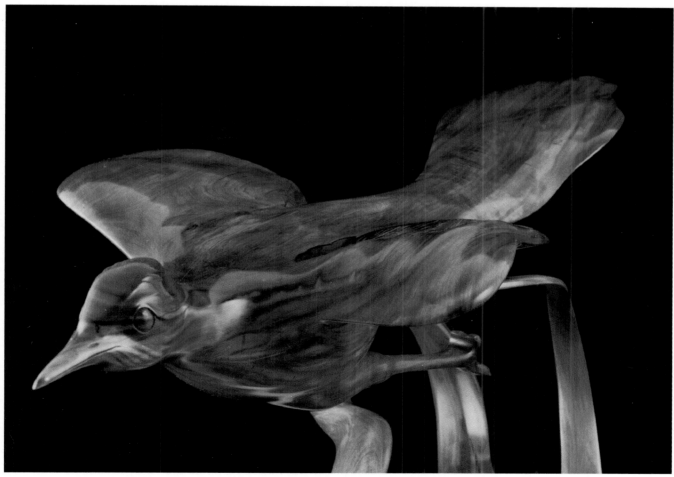

***And we know that the Son of God is come, and hath given us an understanding
that we may know Him that is true . . .***
***I John 5:20***

West Texas Juniper on Mesquite

Height 11″ Length 17 1/2″

# QUINTESSENCE OF FLIGHT

What is the alluring essence of flight that draws a human heart to be almost covetous of this ability, and what spiritual truth could God illustrate with such an intriguing picture? *"He that hath my commandments, and keepeth them, he it is that loveth me . . . "* (John 14:21) Could it be that our problems with keeping His commands stem from a lack of love for Jesus? God will not place His finger on a problem without making a solution available. *We love because He first loved us"* (I John 4:19). As an eagle is designed to fly leaping out from its perch high above the canyon floor and stretching forth its wings, so we are designed to respond to the revelation of God's love by loving Him in return.

After having this truth brought to mind through a book, I began to follow the author's advice, "Pray God to reveal His love to you, so that you might love Him more." Waiting in faith for God to answer this prayer brought about a beautiful revelation triggered by two simple words, *My Jesus.*

Jesus has given Himself to each of us much like a husband gives himself to his wife, only in a perfect way—a total commitment. *All* thoughts and desires are fixed on us as individuals. Scripture puts it this way. *"I am my beloved's and my beloved is mine . . ."* (Song of Solomon 6:3). The revelation was of His person given to me—unfeigned, undivided, unending. As the old hymn puts it, I saw *Jesus, Lover of my soul.* How Jesus gives each of us His all is beyond me. He is God, and with God all things are possible. The picture He painted was this: I could struggle and scramble over obstacles here on earth in an effort to do His will, or I could soar on wings of love as I focused on Who it is that loves me and what that love can do.

Isaiah 40:31    I John 4:19    Song of Solomon 6:3

*What strength I find*
*on eagle's wing*
*as now my heart*
*does soar and sing,*
*to know my Savior's*
*gift to me*
*was more than just*
*to set me free.*

*More than a love*
*as vast as space*
*or gifts of power,*
*strength and grace,*
*the thing that shakes*
*my heart today*
*is that I finally*
*heard Him say,*

*"I died and gave*
*my life that's true;*
*but now I give*
*my Self to you."*

*But they that wait upon the Lord shall renew their strength; they shall mount up with wings as eagles; they shall run, and not be weary; and they shall walk, and not faint.*
**Isaiah 40:31**

West Texas Juniper on Walnut Base

Wingspan 41″

# STANDARD CHRISTIANITY
## (A Semblance of a Scissortail)

As a child I heard that the scissortail will fly by and clip your hair off to build her nest. But since I wore a burr haircut, I knew I was safe from the little varments.

The scissortail flycatcher bears only a semblance to his namesake, nothing more. That is really the only point that ties this sculpture with the following poem. I pray that the above point never may be applicable to anyone who bears the name Christian, yet to varying degrees we all fall short of the standard Jesus raised and ever lives to help us attain.

I recently read a book about the Scottish Covenantors. The short testimonies of these men and women shook me. For the cause of Christ, they lived in the woods of Scotland, hunted like animals. Once caught, they were tortured and either exiled or killed. The stories detailed the horrors they suffered, but also recorded their last words and the sermons they were allowed to give on the gallow steps. They showed no regret for the life they were losing, but with radiant hearts embraced *the Life* who so evidently stood at their sides.

My heart ached to know Jesus in the way they so clearly knew Him. It was then that I saw I had a choice to make. As long as I held onto my inferior *prize*, it would inhibit that type of relationship. Paul warned us not to follow an unwise path: *"For we dare not make ourselves of the number, or compare ourselves with some that commend themselves: but they measuring themselves by themselves, and comparing themselves among themselves, are not wise"* (II Corinthians 10:12). So often I have ignored that warning and continued to try and stay one step ahead of my Christian peers; but being the lead turtle in a turtle race still does not get you anywhere fast.

The standard raised in the American Church, so often falls way short of the one Jesus offers us. By attaining to that standard, I have continued to cling desperately to my *prize* of comforts and securities so that I have no room in my hands for the glories that come from an abandoned acceptance of God's will for me. I am not alone in this spiritually impoverished race. So I ask for prayer, not only for myself, but for the American Church, that we no longer will allow ourselves to be robbed of the riches of Christ Jesus. May we no longer pitch our camp on the brink of the fatal cliff of *"friendship* [with] *the world"* (James 4:4); instead may we see through the eyes of eternity and *"set our affection on things above, not on things on the earth"* (Colossians 3:2), and walk worthy of *"the high calling of God in Jesus Christ"* (Philippians 3:14).

II Corinthians 10:12

Philippians 1:20

Philippians 3:14

Colossians 3:2

James 4:4

*A weak and wavering standard*
  *is being raised as a Christian flag;*
*for a depth and life and suffering*
  *this gilded mask does lag.*
*Measured by securities,*
  *our comforts and our smiles,*
*is this superficial Christianity*
  *where hangnails rate as trials.*

*Oh my God, forgive me*
  *for receiving not the pain;*
*You agonized upon the cross*
  *that I be born again.*
*And for thinking I deserve*
  *the riches of this earth*
*as my part of Thy inheritance*
  *that comes with that new birth.*

*The riches and the blessings,*
  *the comforts and the gains,*
*are **Yours** to give, I have no right*
  *to at **my** leisure claim.*
*I have one right,*
  *to lay it **all** completely at Your feet,*
*to receive in humble gratitude*
  *what **You** deem makes me complete.*

*Whether pain and tribulation*
  *or the joy Your presence gives.*
***You** define the blessings;*
  ***You** decide what lives.*

*My heart seeks, Lord, at times to bow*
  *toward the throne of selfish gain;*
*my prayer, Most High, is when it does,*
  *I writhe in burning pain*
*'til finally I learn a joy*
  *existing foreign to this world,*
*and with a thankful heart for "Thy will be done"*
  *the true standard is unfurled.*

**According to my earnest expectation and my hope, that in nothing I shall be ashamed,**
**but that with all boldness, as always, so now also Christ shall be magnified**
**in my body, whether it be by life, or by death.**
**Philippians 1:20**

West Texas Juniper
Height 14″

# CAST THY BURDENS

*I don't know what to do, God. You expect me to know what to do. I don't know what to do, I don't even know what to pray. There's too much to pray about, I don't know where to begin. They're starving down here—spiritually and physically. They're lost and miserable and they're everywhere, just everywhere. Look! You pray, God. I've had it, simply had it. You pray, God . . . Oh God, please I need You. Please God, I need you . . .*

These last words trailed off in an anguished sob, the only intelligent thing I had said all day. Was God the Father offended to hear the angry words He so clearly could see within my heart, He who desires truth in the inward parts? The hurt was there; speaking it forth let me see just what was inside hurting. The burdens of mission work weighed too heavy upon my prideful heart. Under my own strength I could take no other step, but one—to humble myself . . . casting all my cares upon Him. This was God's clear cry for action, not merely attitude—a call to step into His grace.

The Lord then said to me: *Son, you're not down there to carry those burdens, but to lift the needs up to Me. Place them in My hand and trust Me to do My part. Believe Me and rest assured . . .*

Memories of my newborn niece resting on my chest came to mind. Never had I seen anyone so helpless, yet never had I met a more secure individual. Clearly she had not a worry in the world. What security! Was she consciously trusting?

God calls us to enter into His rest, that total childlike trust in Him. As with the children of Israel in the desert, unbelief—focusing on our ability or inability instead of on Jesus and His character and ability—can keep us from the promised land of His rest. We must cast off the weeds that choke us from following Him and cast all our cares upon Him, for He cares for us. Then and only then will our hearts be free to serve Him.

*For he that is entered into his rest, he also hath ceased from his own works, as God did from his.* **Hebrews 4:10**

Hebrews 3:8-19, 4:1-12     Mark 4:7,19     Luke 8:7,14     Hebrews 12:1

Father, I am Your child
   yet I'm tangled in these snares,
trying to produce good fruit,
   but weighted down with cares.

Studying Your Word
   which has taken such strong root,
striving more to see the truth,
   but just tasting of the fruit.

Father, all I want
   is to fill my heart with You,
to know Your will and do it,
   for my actions to be true.

Jesus, in Your Word
   You say Your burden's light,
so please explain this heaviness
   upon my heart tonight.

Even though I grumble
   and frustration moves this pen,
You ask me to come unto You
   to praise You once again.

And now I see the cares are small,
   You'll take them from my arms
as I lay upon Your gentle chest,
   safe from all that harms.

*Humble yourselves therefore under the mighty hand of God, that he may exalt you in due time:*
*Casting all your care upon him; for he careth for you.*
**I Peter 5:6-7**

West Texas Juniper and Mesquite

Height 21″

# THE ONE YOU KNOW

Picture someone you consider a wise person. You may think of someone like Socrates, or perhaps a personal acquaintance comes to mind. What constitutes the criterion you use for judging a person as wise: age, honesty, success, respectability, stability or intelligence? Maybe they simply have workable solutions for life's daily dilemmas.

In this sculpture, I try to depict Socrates as he holds the fatal vial of hemlock in his hand. What were the last thoughts of this *wise mind*? Did he examine his life and philosophies? Did he wonder: *What if there really is a God of judgement?* Did God in His mercy show him the vanity of fame, fortune, honor and knowledge void of God? What would it have taken to pull the prideful scales from his eyes and allow him to reach out in faith to a loving God who desired to save his soul?

The question: *"For what shall it profit a man, if he shall gain the whole world, and lose his own soul?"* (Mark 8:36) might seem cruel to ask a person in Socrates' position. Yet it would be mercy.

Often the wise of this world fail to listen to *foolish* Christians and our claims of a much better world beyond the grave. They scoff at claims of actually knowing God, Jesus Christ, in a real and personal way. Their deafened ears can't hear the whisper of our mere words. They need to *see* Jesus in our actions, for actions speak louder than words. As we love God, one another and them, they will begin to see in our words the true explanation of the light they see shining clearly through us to a dark, uncaring world. Then they will finally release their grip on this world and ask to meet the One you know.

Philippians 2:14-15     I Timothy 4:12

*The aged and wise oft' realize*
*the folly of their ways,*
*of spending life a searching*
*without Jesus in their days.*

*The history of their life*
*is etched upon their face,*
*times of joy, peace and love,*
*failure and disgrace.*

*Respected as they are*
*for their many works and age,*
*God's presence isn't given count*
*by these ones so very "sage."*

*So all their works are ashes,*
*all their joy shall end*
*when they cross that final barrier,*
*the spirit world transcend.*

*Yet there's a ray of hope and light*
*despite their many years;*
*Jesus Christ still loves them,*
*has been saving all their tears.*

*The prayers of all their loved ones*
*will be answered 'fore they go.*
*When they see Christ's love shine through you*
*and ask to meet the One you know.*

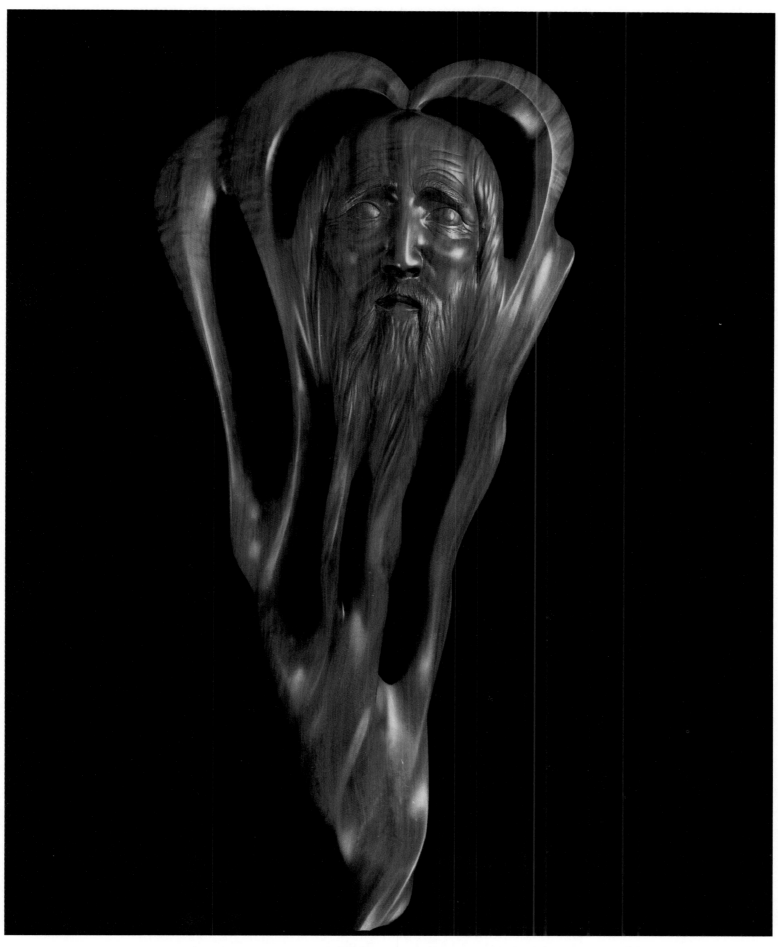

*Do all things without murmurings and disputings: That ye may be blameless and harmless, the sons of God, without rebuke, in the midst of a crooked and perverse nation, among whom ye shine as lights in the world.*
**Philippians 2:14-16**

West Texas Juniper

Height 28″

# OUR WINGS HIS GIFTS OF GRACE

Gravity is an inescapable reality. Or is it? As constant and unforgiving as gravity is, there are other laws that, if followed, free us from the limitations imposed on us by gravity. For example, if the laws of lift are applied correctly, a ton of steel can fly across a continent filled with formerly earthbound passengers. Design, momentum and control all work together to fulfill the law of lift and keep an airplane flying. Yet all three must be maintained in order to thwart gravity's pull.

That illustration gives us a picture of the truth about two other laws, these being in the spiritual realm. Who could deny the ever present tug of sin: "me first." It is as constant as gravity, keeping us self-bound when our hearts yearn to soar in the realms of selfless giving. Yet there is a law that supersedes the law of sin and death. *"For the law of the Spirit of life in Christ Jesus hath made me free from the law of sin and death"* (Romans 8:2). An allegorical paraphrase might read like this: For the law of lift in Christ Jesus has made me free from the law of gravity. God has made a way to walk in victory over sin (walking in the spirit), but we so often lose sight of that simple way and fall prey to the trap of trying *not to walk* after the flesh.

The formula for the law of lift parallels in this manner. As one is born into the kingdom of God through faith in Jesus Christ, he is "designed to fly." *"But as many as received him, to them gave he the power to become the sons of God . . ."* (John 1:12) We are led of His Spirit to obey His commands. *"For as many as are led by the Spirit of God, they are the sons of God"* (Romans 8:14). If we allow the Spirit of God to lead and instruct, and we obey His leading, our lives are very simply *spirit controlled.* Since Jesus promised that the Holy Spirit would lead us into all truth (John 16:13), we have the assurance by His promise of being led into victory. Our momentum, or what moves us, comes from the heart's desire to know Him. Paul, the apostle, told us that was his highest desire in life: *"That I many know Him . . ."* (Philippians 3:10) And we see how those three things working together allowed God to use Paul to turn the world upside down. Through the guidance of the Holy Spirit, our efforts to know Jesus will result in obedience to His commands, victory over sin and a motivation to know Him in an ever deeper way. However, all these things should stem from and lead back to faith and trust—faith in His promises and trust in His character. These are our wings, His gifts to us; but they only work when we stretch them out and go.

Romans 8:2      Galatians 5:16      II Peter 1:14

*An eagle doesn't take the air*
*    by trying **not** to fall,*
*but graciously pursues the task,*
*    high above it all.*
*By using what's provided*
*    he fulfills the law of lift,*
*pursues his food or builds a nest*
*    on wings both strong and swift.*

*So how can we expect to see*
*    a victory over sin,*
*if we go through life with eyes upon*
*    the mortal ills within,*
*instead of fixing firmly*
*    our eyes upon His face,*
*pursuing God through faith and trust,*
*    our wings His gifts of grace.*

*But I say, walk and live [habitually] in the [Holy] Spirit [responsive to and controlled
and guided by the Spirit]; then you will certainly not gratify the cravings
and desires of the flesh (of human nature without God).*
**Galatians 5:16 AB**

West Texas Juniper

Wingspan 35″

# POLLY IS A CHRISTIAN

If you have ever heard and understood the expression "Polly wants a cracker," then the point brought home by this poem and sculpture needs little explanation. True, parrots can associate phrases with reward, but the real understanding of what they are saying escapes their little, feathered heads. They end up repeating the question rather than formulating an answer. Unfortunately, this sad phenomenon occurs among humans when an understanding beyond their capacity is required for the response.

Hebrews 11:3 states, *"Through faith we understand that the worlds were framed by the word of God..."* Mere head knowledge and a conditioned response, whether it is a phrase or a certain behavior, don't add up to true understanding. To God, *why* a person says and does things is of much more importance than *what* a person says and does. Read First Corinthians 13:1-4 if you need evidence of that, or consider Jesus' response to the *outward* piety of the Pharisees. Our Lord looks on the intents and motives of the heart, knowing that it is out of the abundance of the heart that the mouth speaks.

If He can change the heart, the person's outward conversation is altered as well. Faith in Him is the vehicle of change. But I really don't need to build a big case to prove this point. All of us have seen (or been) the hypocrite who *faithfully* perches on a pew each Sunday, has a spiritual vocabulary of seventeen scriptures, and squawks a good amen at the proper moments, and then lives a life from Monday through Saturday that unmistakeably reveals a heart that knows nothing of the selfless, giving love of the God he *serves*. In any given town in America, the members of "First Cockatoo Assembly" would probably outnumber the true saints of God. Is it any wonder that poor lost souls won't listen to a gospel that is so inconsistent with the life of the speaker? Talking to a parrot is a novel thrill, but who would seriously invest in a bird's advice?

Parrot a phrase,
   can that make you whole;
do syllables spoken
   or deeds save your soul?

You know all the words,
   and the movements as well,
but the reasons they're spoken
   you can't even tell.

They hold no true meaning
   so you would never conceive
of doing these things
   you say you believe

and can't understand
   a man's fervent desire
to leave the things of this world
   for those unseen that are higher.

Pity the parrot,
   though he speaks and is heard,
no one truly listens
   to the thoughts of a bird.

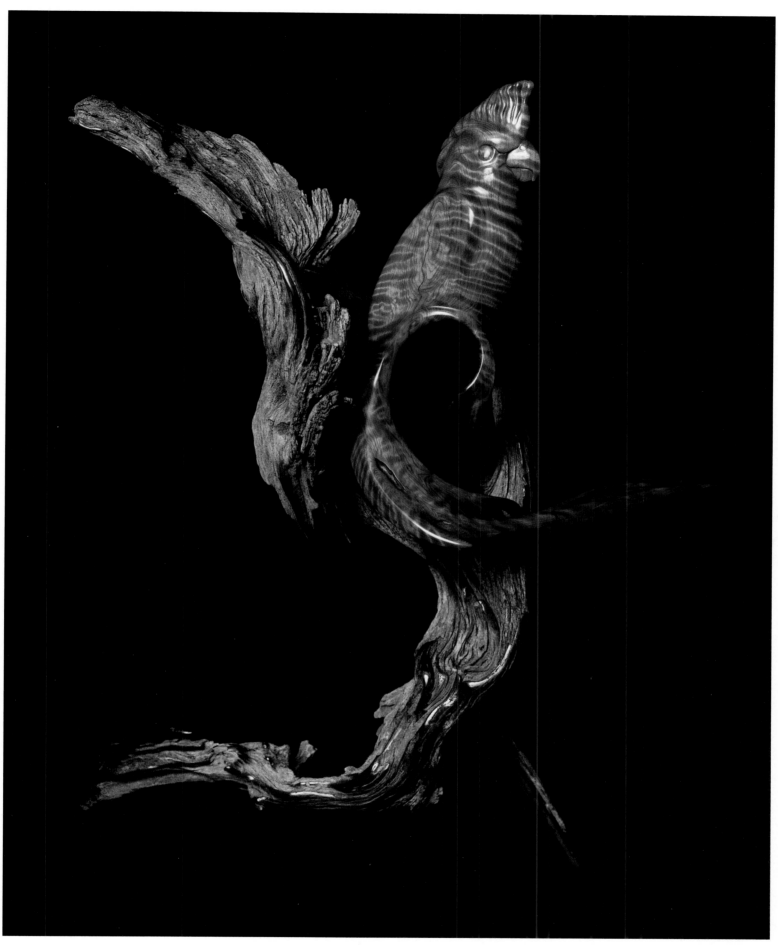

***For with the heart man believeth unto righteousness . . .***
**Romans 10:10**

West Texas Juniper on Mesquite
Height 27″

# TO COVER OUR SHAME

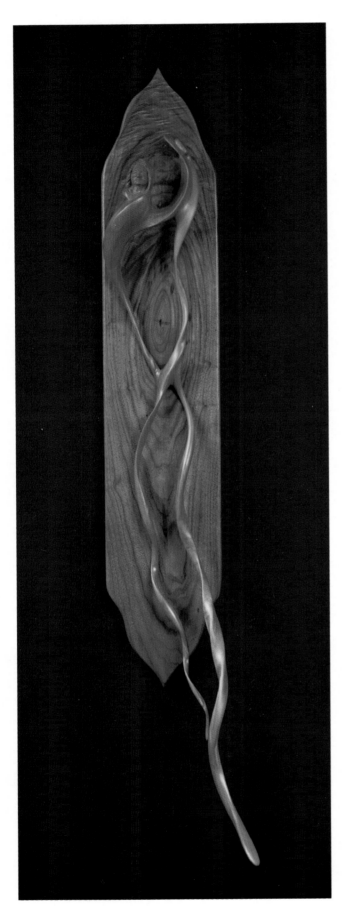

Though this sculpture was finished in 1979, the accompanying poem wasn't written until the summer of 1985. The sculpture did have a poem all those years to explain Eve's posture and the presence of the serpent with his shadowy influence cast across her head, but it was written by someone under the delusion that he was a Christian when, in fact, he didn't truly know what a Christian was. I was trying to relate truth from the Word of God when I had never met the Truth.

The Word of God in a man's heart, without faith, produces no more true understanding than a dunk in the lake helps a cat to understand a fish's love of water. Since we are designed to dwell in God's Kingdom, the problems arise not from what's missing but from what's been added to our hearts, unbelief. Trust comes without thought in the world of a much loved baby. The love of the parents communicates everything to the little babe. It was this same *life* of faith and trust that Adam and Eve chose to exchange for unbelief and the thin dry air of death.

Though we, too, are kept from the garden through unbelief, a loving Father made a door for us to enter His fullness again. The door is Jesus Christ, and we enter in by faith in Him.

*The just shall live by faith.* **Romans 1:17**

*I am the door; by me if any man enter in, he shall be saved, and shall go in and out, and find pasture.* **John 10:9**

What was the sin
   of God's daughter, Eve?
Put quite simply,
   she didn't believe
the things God had spoken
   to her by His Word;
she would know **more**
   than the things she had heard.

So she heard the serpent
   and believed his untruth,
that the Word of the Lord
   needed some proof,
and exercised wisdom
   of the base foolish kind,
as rebellious fingers
   touched forbidden rind.

We can't, as with Eve,
   our nakedness hide,
for in rebellion and sin
   we also abide;
but God in His mercy
   made a way through His Son
to wipe clean our slate,
   to repair what was done.

So lay down "your" efforts
   to add to the cross;
take God at His Word
   and count all other loss.

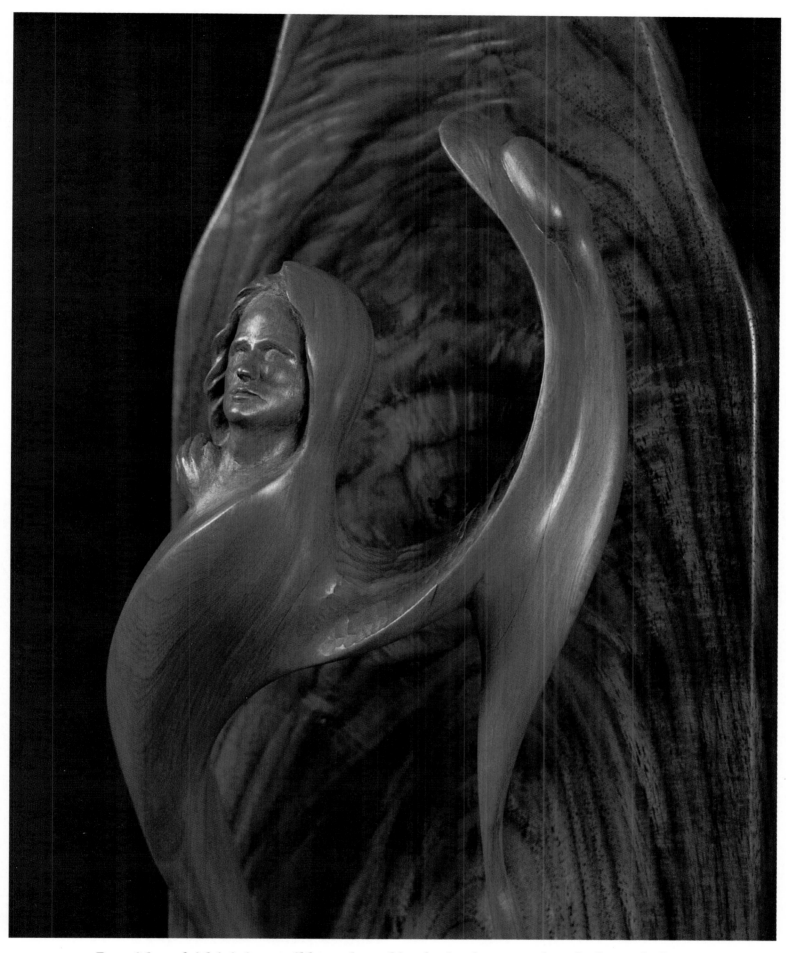

*But without faith it is impossible to please him: for he that cometh to God must believe that he is, and that he is a rewarder of them that diligently seek him.*
**Hebrews 11:6**

West Texas Juniper on Walnut

Height 35″

# BABEL'S FOLLY

*And the whole earth was of one language, and of one speech. And it came to pass, as they journeyed from the east, that they found a plain in the land of Shinar; and they dwelt there. And they said one to another, Go to, let us make brick, and burn them throughly. And they had brick for stone, and slime had they for morter. And they said, Go to, let us build us a city and a tower, whose top may reach unto heaven; and let us make a name, lest we be scattered abroad upon the face of the whole earth.*

*And the Lord came down to see the city and the tower, which the children of men builded. And the Lord said, Behold the people is one, and they have all one language; and this they began to do: and now nothing will be restrained from them, which they have imagined to do.* **Genesis 11:1-6**

In the twentieth century, the ruins of the Tower of Babel are found along the old banks of the Euphrates River, and the folly of Babel is found to be repeating itself time and again. The people of ancient Babylon were able to perform what they imagined because of God-given abilities and a unity achieved through the vehicle of one common language. With the advent of computers, one language is again being spoken over all the earth. At one time scientific knowledge doubled every one hundred years; with the help of the computer, it now doubles every three months. Knowledge is not bad; it's what we do with knowledge, our wisdom, that suffers lack.

Scientific knowledge is intended to reveal God and His Kingdom. We, through ingratitude, choose not to see Him in His creations. Then, in our striving to achieve what only God can achieve in our lives, we become blind and . . .

*Professing themselves to be wise, they became fools . . .* **Romans 1:22**

With feet planted firmly
  on a perilous spire,
the children of men
  would strive to go higher,
by questing for answers
  who's origins stem
from a misguided helmsman,
  the science of men.

True he has made wings
  with which to fly,
but they limit us still
  to the realms of the sky,
and focus our eyes
  on intellect's lie
that on our own strength and effort
  we'll surely get by.

Yet with what we are "given,"
  try as we may
to the "giver" of all
  we can never repay
one single moment
  we recklessly spoil
through efforts of climbing
  our towers of soil.

**It is better to trust in the Lord than to put confidence in man.**
**Psalms 118:8**

West Texas Juniper on Mesquite
Height 30″

# DOUBTER'S WEB

A very important act of faith was the precipitator of the event that led to this poem. Within hours of giving my life to Jesus and relinquishing control (being my own boss), a still small voice began asking me to do a seemingly foolish task. Though I was not convinced of the source of the small voice, I set out to obey. Was it God's voice? Does He really still speak to people? The voice told me to *take a hike* (great first words to hear from a loving Father)! Yet, the hike became such a joy and adventure that I didn't really want to hear the second request—*Time to go home.* When I looked toward home and the rapidly approaching thunderstorm, I made an assessment and a decision: *I don't care if this voice is God, my imagination or the devil. I believe it to be God and I am going to trust Him and obey.* Instantly, the vacuum in my chest broke; the dry, empty hurting began to be filled, and joy poured in as longing and loneliness were driven out. After years of seeking, I finally had found it.

Baffled cattle wondered at the whooping, laughing human who seemingly had been driven into the storm. They couldn't understand that he was being led; he had finally escaped the Doubter's Web.

*. . . if ye continue in my word, then are ye my disciples indeed; And ye shall know the truth, and the truth shall make you free.* **John 8:31-32**

*But wilt thou know, o vain man, that faith without works is dead?* **James 2:20**

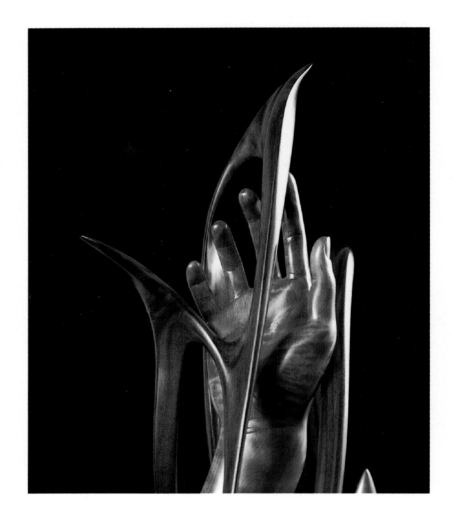

*Of all things from the devil*
    *doubt's by far the worst,*
*for it steals away your faith,*
    *the thing you must have first*

*to combat all forms of evil*
    *and defeat them in Christ's name;*
*doubt can make believing*
    *a long and fruitless game.*

*Many people have strong faith,*
    *at least that's what they say,*
*but they wait to act upon it,*
    *'till they find a better day.*

*If you don't act, you don't believe,*
    *or else you'd have no fear*
*to do the things the Bible says*
    *today and not next year.*

*So reach up for the Kingdom,*
    *watch your efforts wane and ebb,*
*until you act upon the Word*
    *and escape the doubter's web.*

*But be ye doers of the word, and not hearers only, deceiving your own selves.*
**James 1:22**

West Texas Juniper and Mesquite

Height 14″

# SHEER IMPOSSIBILITY

If ever a beam of light decided to warmly embrace a poor cold shadow, try as it may, its desires could never be realized. The very nature of light destroys darkness, the absence of light. A loving God would never violate our rights by changing our very nature against our will, but He would provide a way for us to change if we so desired.

Jesus stated, *"He that believeth on him is not condemned: but he that believeth not is condemned already, because he hath not believed in the name of the only begotten Son of God. And this is the condemnation, that light is come into the world, and men loved darkness rather than light, because their deeds were evil"* (John 3:18-19).

To step into the light, we must be **willing** to have our old nature completely destroyed and totally changed. That is the attitude of repentance. Belief is trusting in Jesus with the whole heart—His finished work at Calvary and His ability to accomplish that change—and **then** stepping into the light. The realization that we do not have light of our own draws us to the light and love of the Father. As we are born of His Spirit through the way He provided, Jesus Christ, we begin to understand and assume His nature, and He begins to shine through us.

*Therefore if any man be in Christ* **[the light of the world]**, *he is a new creature; old things are passed away; behold, all things are become new.* **I Corinthians 5:17**

Sooner could a fish
   live high up in a tree,
or perhaps a climbing cat
   dwell deep beneath the sea,

than a man
   made out of sod
live in Paradise
   with God,

lest the man
   be born again
and washed spotless
   from his sin.

Lest the man
   be born again
and washed spotless
   from his sin,

he is but
   a shadow soul,
but one died
   to make him whole,

where he can live and breathe
   in light so truly pure,
the very light of God,
   in which no darkness can endure.

***Whereby are given unto us exceeding great and precious promises: that by these ye might be partakers
of the divine nature, having escaped the corruption that is in the world through lust.***
**II Peter 1:4**

Mesquite on Juniper Burl

Height 13″

# A DUCK'S BAFFLE

Do you ever wonder or ponder deep questions? Questions like, Which came first, the verb *duck* or the noun *duck*?

Experiences trigger our wonderful minds to probe and inquire, or at least they should. What direction we take and how deep we probe depends on many things. Before I get to sounding too much like a high brow, I'd better explain about the duck. Back in my *tepee living days,* a friend and I were out early one morning *gathering. Gathering* is a primitive form of *work* that includes hunting food, firewood, wire or anything else that could be useful in one's existence in the wild. As we neared the top of a ravine, my friend yelled, "Duck." I reacted as if it were a command and, just in time, saw a stick swing past and strike a duck out of the air. Had I looked up and asked, "Oh really, where?" I would have had a duck batted down my throat. Dinner would have been early and I would have missed a perfectly good model for this sculpture. *Gathering* completed, I set about a different form of duck hunting, with hatchet and saw in hand. Very shortly before the model reached an inedible condition, I had a wooden similitude of a duck.

The question I wish to ask is this: What do we see in God's creations? Can we ever exhaust the knowledge obtainable from even the smallest of them? Why do we stop at the superficial level or, worse yet, cease to wonder?

*Because that, when they knew God, they glorified him not as God, neither were thankful; but became vain in their imaginations, and their foolish heart was darkened. Professing themselves to be wise, they became fools, and changed the glory of the incorruptible God into an image made like to corruptible man . . . Romans 1:21-23*

*Paddling along*
*    content as can be,*
*the place of your destiny*
*    you cannot see,*

*for your world's enough*
*    though the waves get you down,*
*never a moment*
*    do you think you might drown.*

*Little by little*
*    the seasons do change;*
*so you, as always,*
*    your life rearrange;*

*don't face the issues,*
*    don't face the cold;*
*turn once more your back,*
*    flee the truth when it's told.*

*Why question the clockwork*
*    that governs this world*
*or examine the reason*
*    why through darkness it's hurled,*

*it's so much easier*
*    to just be a duck*
*eyes pointed southward*
*    in ignorance stuck.*

*I do not frustrate the grace of God: for if righteousness come by the law,*
*then Christ is dead in vain.*
**Galatians 2:21**

West Texas Juniper on Mesquite

Height 10″

# THE TRUTH REMAINS

Red sandstone walls rise in majestic splendor out of green wooded slopes; cactus, junipers, muledeer and the elusive audad sheep are but a part of the make-up of the maze of canyons called Palo-Duro. The dark fingers of the narrow side-canyons create a stark contrast as they reach into the treeless plains of the Texas Panhandle. Seep-springs and streams in verdant green soothe eyes wearied by the endless expanse of the dusty brown horizon.

I could describe a scene until words failed me, but if you gazed upon the same view, my words would cease to be the vehicle needed to carry the sights of the canyon to the eye of your mind. One picture is truly worth a thousand words. Although I can explain to you a concept of truth, experiencing that truth brings a much deeper and richer revelation of what is being said. For example, I can tell you of beauty, but you can clearly see the truth of my words by looking at a rose. *"For the invisible things of him from the creation of the world are clearly seen, being understood by the things that are made, even his eternal power and Godhead"* (Romans 1:20). It's when we cease to recognize God as God and cease to be thankful, that we lose sight of Him in His creation. He has made a way for us to clearly see Him again.

I used to walk those canyons in search of God; I now walk those same majestic ledges with their very Maker, thankfully aware of a Beauty far beyond the realm of sight.

***For the invisible things of him from the creation of the world are clearly seen, being understood by the things that are made, even his eternal power and godhead, so that they are without excuse.*** Romans 1:20

*Canyon walls*
*    of red and green*
*paint more for us*
*    than just a scene,*

*with everything*
*    that's e'er been made*
*a truth foundation*
*    has been laid.*

*The Maker's hand*
*    one can detect*
*by giving Him*
*    His due respect,*

*and thanking Him*
*    for His loving grace*
*that enables us*
*    to seek His face.*

*So from the sheep*
*    what can we see*
*as He blends into*
*    the rocks and trees?*

*The greatest truth*
*    that's e'er been said,*
*"a Lamb once slain*
*    has raised the dead."*

**_The next day John seeth Jesus coming unto him, and saith, Behold the Lamb of God,_**
**_which taketh away the sin of the world._**
**John 1:29**

West Texas Juniper, Huisache on Mesquite Base

Height 31″

# LOST IN PRIDE

I never really wanted much out of life, other than my independence and the freedom to travel wherever I wanted—to be my own boss, so to speak. Eastern religions had upheld my belief and practice that one became a prisoner to his possessions. Material possessions undesired, all I really lacked in life was my "ticket to travel." That ticket, after years of being a starving artist, finally arrived in the form of a firm market for my sculptures. Now I had it, everything I wanted; now I was happy.

I thought it a horrible shame at the time, but now I see it as an act of mercy from God, because there was one gift from God that was suddenly taken away: the ability to receive satisfaction and fulfillment from the other gifts He had given me. *"Also, every man to whom God has given riches and possessions, and power to enjoy them and to accept his appointed lot and to rejoice in his toil—this is the gift of God* [to him]*"* (Ecclesiastes 5:19, AB).

God did give me a gift to replace the one removed, a revelation: *Nothing in this world is going to fulfill you and make you happy.* I found myself inadvertently quoting King Solomon, *"Vanity of vanities . . . all is vanity"* (Ecclesiastes 1:2).

An acute awareness of a need for *something more* arose. My years of searching seemed all in vain. What more could there be that I hadn't tried? Empty, void, tasteless, these words all fell short in their efforts to describe the immense gulf that lay ahead. *With my luck, I'll probably live to be ninety-five, seventy more years of **having it all**, great. I gave 'er my best shot, and it's a dead-end; I'm lost.* Praise God, I was **lost**, but not forsaken.

This sculpture contains a very distinct cross at its center. Though lost to view in the photo on the next page, the shadow of the cross is clearly seen at the sculpture's side.

*Walking down the paths of life*
*    we wonder how to know,*
*the wheres, the whys, the dos, the don'ts*
*    of how we are to go.*

*And always searching with our minds*
*    for something to be used*
*to make our burden less complete,*
*    our purpose less confused.*

*We pick up one, discard the next*
*    as we reach for still another,*
*mode of transportation*
*    that's more suiting than the other.*

*When all the time we shun the road*
*    that leads to truth forever,*
*we see it oft' times at our side,*
*    yet, to take it we say "never."*

*"Why that road's for fools and hypocrites,*
*    squares and smiling losers;*
*I'd rather walk among the thieves,*
*    the murderers and boozers,*

*than give up my heavy burden*
*    that gets greater every day*
*and say unto the Lord, my God,*
*    "I'm lost, please show the way."*

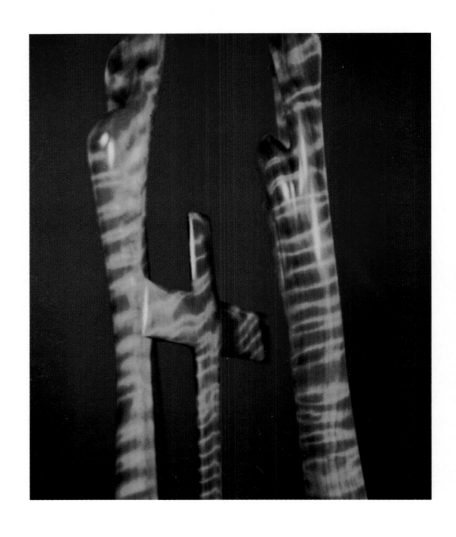

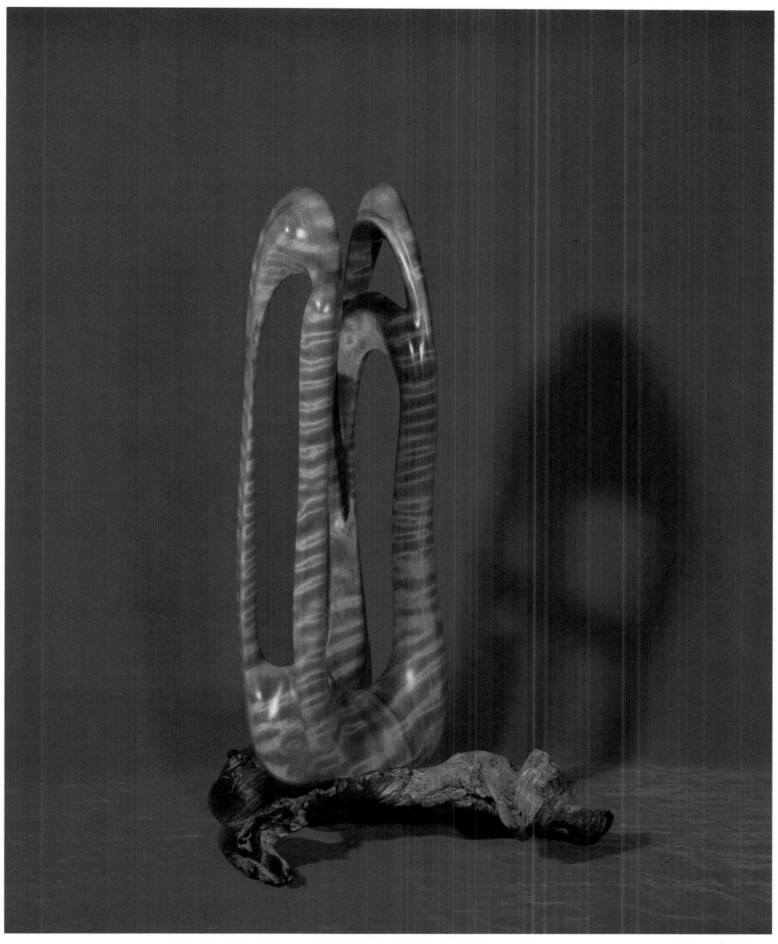

***Jesus saith unto him, I am the way, the truth, and the life: no man cometh
unto the Father, but by me.***
**John 14:6**

West Texas Juniper on Mesquite

Height 14″

# HEART CRY

*But needs be please a way to see, and look beyond the veil,*
*a blind man views through pipes and dreams, but cannot **see** the trail.*

What chance did the native American have against a people who spent most every waking hour bent on possessing as much of this earth as they possibly could? The intrigue and mystery of the American Indian has been a part of my dreams as far back as memory leads me. The people, their beliefs, their lifestyle—so much a part of nature and so *surely on the road to God.* For after all, wasn't nature God's purest expression of Himself? So went my thinking and so went my search. *If snake liver, and hackberries were good enough for Quanah Parker, then they were good enough for me.* Tepee living is just downright comfortable, and buffalo robes make a right smart bed. Fasting, sitting half-naked on the edge of a lonesome plateau and waiting for three days for a revelation from the Great Spirit produced little more than additional questions and a multitude of various insect bites.

What did I find on my search into the life and creeds of the American Plains Indian? I found a people with a spirituality that shames most Christians in the areas of commitment, diligence and discipline—a people who lived life with a conscious effort to know and serve their creator.

How sad that the good news, the path they searched for, came cloaked in robes of self-righteous traditions borne by ambassadors who knew not the nature of their King. I am aware of few Christians who came to these wonderful people with this simple message: The Great Spirit has sent His only begotten Son to answer the cry of your heart.

*Rising each morning*
  *to a God I don't know,*
*the pull in my heart*
  *how it hurts me so.*
*Frustrations arise*
  *as I strive to touch*
*the God who has loved me*
  *and given so much.*

*I know You are there*
  *beckoning me,*
*but, oh my eyes*
  *just cannot see.*
*Open my heart,*
  *please make a way*
*where stumbling in darkness*
  *gives place to day.*

*You're God of all the universe,*
  *God of here below;*
*You're mighty and good*
  *and this thing I know,*
*if You can make an eagle fly*
  *in realms of vibrant blue,*
*You can make a way for man*
  *to love and come to know You.*

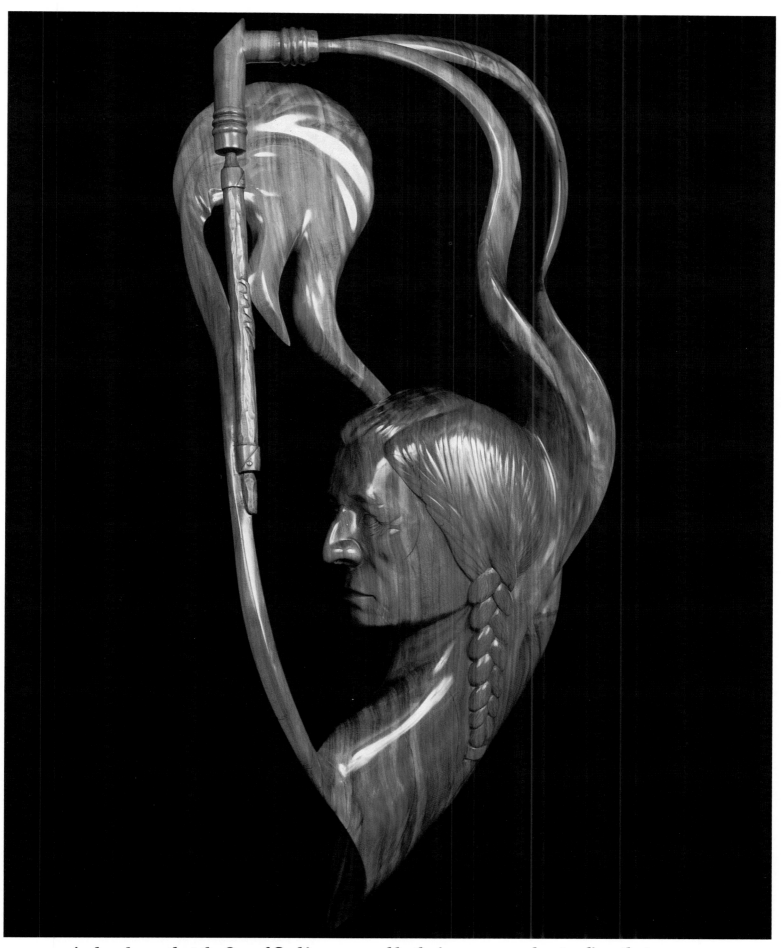

*And we know that the Son of God is come, and hath given us an understanding, that we may know him that is true, and we are in him that is true even his Son Jesus Christ.*
*This is the true God, and eternal life.*
**I John 5:20**

West Texas Juniper

7/8 Life-Size

Height 27″

# ABOUT THE WOOD

The golden-colored wood in these sculptures is West Texas juniper (juniperus texensis Van Mull). The only place in the world it grows is along a stretch of cliffs in the Texas Panhandle, ranging from north of Amarillo to near Big Spring, Texas. This juniper is the densest juniper known, approximately 44 pounds per cubic foot.

By hiking through the canyons, I am able to examine hundreds of dead-standing and fallen trees in an effort to select one that fits the idea I desire to carve. Since many portions of the canyons provided the firewood and fence posts used during the early 1900's, most of the really big dead trees are found where the cedar cutters could not get a mule or a fool to go. I have always felt like God left those especially for me.

The dark wood in most of the sculptures is what I call black mesquite. Mesquite, if left in the ground long enough, will eventually turn as black as ebony (at least what is left of the wood will). To find the dark wood takes a lot of looking, but, when polished, it is well worth the effort.

Hopefully, you have gleaned from the writing above that the challenge to make one of these sculptures does not begin once the wood is strapped to the work table. By that point it has already been proven to me in many ways that I am merely God's vessel and it is His project, not mine alone.

**Note:** I extend a special thanks to the ranchers who have allowed me to search their ranches for wood and solitude. Thank you so much. I really do appreciate your generosity.

# ABOUT THE TOOLS

During the years I have been carving I have watched many people come up with their praise and compliments. Never once have I seen anyone direct that praise to the iron and steel tools that fashion these trees into images of people, birds and flowing forms. Folks always seem to address the person behind the tools. I suppose they realize that it's the hands, eyes and mind of the artist that direct and guide the tools to do their proper work.

It is my prayer that in like manner people would realize that the artist is but a tool in the hand of God, the supreme Artist and Creator of all things. The skills, ideas and patience required to complete one of these works are merely gifts to be used to His glory. Each sculpture is a work of grace for which I thank my God and Lord, Jesus Christ.

Sequential shots of a sculpture (For the Joy of It, pages 46-47) in progress. Prior to step two was the major undertaking of cutting the log and hauling it out of the canyon.

**Step 2: The initial log, approximately 165 pounds**

**Step 5: Abstract shapes of water beginning to form and first stages of details of the sailfish put in place**

**Step 3: Large chunks removed by bow saw and hatchet**

**Step 6: Details placed and a rasp used to remove gouge marks and true up lines and planes**

**Step 4: Gouge and mallet used to free fish and remove excess wood**

**Step 7: Details refined, sculpture ready for sanding, sitting atop the wood chips removed since Step 2**

# FOR THE JOY OF IT

"Put yourself in her shoes." How deeply are you capable of dwelling on another's circumstances and really feeling his pain or joy? I am sure the answer to that depends on how much time and heart you are willing to invest. Please slow down and invest a few thoughts and moments in the testimony of a simply genuine, good-humored, down-to-earth West Texas farmer's wife—an exceptional example. If you could catch a glimmer of the light cast by the last rays of her life, I can guarantee a worthy return for your time.

The scene was a tiny rural hospital with two somewhat self-conscious Christians coming into a room to pray for a dying stranger. We had prayed at the house for her, hoping God would release the burden and we would not have to do this difficult thing. The result of the prayer at the house was an additional burden to deliver a message to her from the book of Job. I knew bone cancer in its final stages was bad, but I was not prepared to see anyone in such pain. There she was, her every move causing pieces of broken vertebrate to grind against frayed nerves. The right side of her face was paralyzed, but she smiled, raised up a little, and shook our hands. She did not battle against self-pity; that battle won, she fought the pain in an effort to make us feel both comfortable and welcomed. If anyone ever had a license to moan about her circumstances, she did; but she still had something to give, and concerned herself first with giving to the concerns of others. Only when I quoted the words of Job that the Lord had impressed upon my heart to give her, did her laughter turn to tears: *"Though he slay me, yet will I trust him"* (Job 13:15).

Even then, however, her tears were not for herself. After a good cry, she explained her prayer to God: That her passing on would display her trust in God in such a way as to convince her husband that she had passed into the arms of Jesus, not death. I paid her several more visits. The time I invested paid rich dividends. A few weeks after our first visit, with her husband by her side, this dear saint bid her farewells and passed into the eternal embrace of the God she had trusted.

I think also of Jesus' testimony *". . . who for the joy that was set before him endured the cross, despising the shame, and is set down at the right hand of the throne of God"* (Hebrews 12:2).

We are all without excuse when it comes to the sin of self-pity, for we have Someone at our side who understands because He's been there Himself. He is able to make our weakness His strength.

Job 13:15     Hebrews 12:1-7     James 1:2-4


*A heart so full it can't contain*
  *the joy it has, despite the pain,*
*for choices lie with those who grieve;*
  *hold tight to hope, or let it leave.*

*For if the moment rules our life,*
  *we can't see purpose through the strife,*
*nor can we mark the goal ahead,*
  *and listless float in pain instead.*

*Beyond the waters of this sea,*
  *a greater purpose there must be,*
*and once we find the Reason why*
  *we, full of joy, leap for the sky.*

*Can this road to hope marked clearly be*
  *where child and scholar both can see,*
*and so be fair, yet foolish look*
  *for it stems from faith in an ancient book.*

*That speaks of One Who rent the grave,*
  *died on the cross, our souls to save.*
*Who daily gives this blessed hope*
  *His strength, His joy, with which we cope.*

*Looking unto Jesus the author and finisher of our faith; who for the joy that was set before him endured the cross, despising the shame, and is set down at the right hand of the throne of God. For consider him . . .*
**Hebrews 12:2-3**

West Texas Juniper on Black Walnut

Height 31″

# DESPERATELY A NEED

Do you recognize that look? Do you ever wear that expression of an injured heart? It happens; men hurt women, sometimes intentionally, but most often they ignorantly strike a chord that pains a woman's soul. Why? Ignorance of design on both parts. Men and women are simply very different, and failure to see the differences leads to pain, unfulfilled expectations, confusion and resentment. Life teaches that at a young age. The solution includes understanding the differences. Scripture provides a clear illustration. *"We love him because he first loved us"* (I John 4:19). We humans are designed to return God's love, not manufacture it. When we try to *return* God's love by *loving Him* under our own power, we fall back under the law, and obeying God becomes a dreary chore. In order truly to be able to love Him back, we need the clear expression of His unconditional love that fosters trust and a desire to please. First John 3:16 shows how this process begins and what our response should be: *"Hereby perceive we the love of God, because he laid down His life for us: and we ought to lay down our lives for the brethren."*

A loving husband laying down his life for his wife, and her response of trust and a desire to bless and please him are given as visual aids for a clearer understanding of our love relationship with God. God, in His Word, admonishes (commands) the husband several times to *"love your wife;"* but He never says, "Wife, *love* your husband." Why this apparent over-balance? First, God wants to get the ball rolling. Since it's not the woman's position to initiate but to respond to a man's expression of his love for her, God has given the man the responsibility to shine the light of His love to his wife. She, like a mirror, reflects it back to him so that he, in turn, may realize the nature of that love and the God who gives it. Secondly, since men don't experience the painful emptiness of neglect with the intensity women do, they tend to forget women's needs or assume her needs are the same as his. Therefore, in His Word, God frequently admonishes the husband to love his wife.

One thing is very certain. If we understand one another's needs, we are much better equipped to meet them. But let us also remember that we must be motivated to search out this understanding through communication with God and one another. Problems left untended grow worse. This is a tender subject that desperately needs addressing, hence the title of the poem.

**Note:** A word to the wise:

Husbands: *don't wait* for an explanation of how it all works *before* you *act* in obedience to God's commands. They are after all commands, not merely suggestions.

Wives: Remember that First Peter, chapter three, was written to women with heathen husbands who valued them less than slaves. It's difficult, but trust God and obey His commands. They are given for your sake.

***Husbands love your wives, even as Christ also loved the church, and gave himself for it . . . So ought men to love their wives as their own bodies . . . Wives, submit yourselves unto your own husbands, as unto the Lord.*** **Ephesians 5:22,25,28**

I Peter 3:1-17      Ephesians 5:22-33

You desperate wounded look
    what's brought you to her face?
I can't explain her actions,
    won't someone plead my case?

For once again I've hurt her,
    cut her deeply, Lord knows how.
She's brooding o'er her secret wound;
    I can't speak with her now.


Why can't he see within my soul
    and sense my simple needs,
to nourish me with attentiveness
    as his own flesh he so feeds;

to ask me what's important
    and acknowledge my attempt
to make his home a castle?
    On my love he pours contempt.


My children; you must understand
    a woman has her way
to meet her husband's deepest needs:
    she's to honor and obey.

But men so need reminding
    what's important in her life,
that nine times in My Word I say,
    "Husband, love your wife."

Husband, give yourself to her
    the expanses of your heart;
for how can she submit to one
    she only owns in part?

**Hereby perceive we the love of God, because he laid down his life for us:
and we ought to lay down our lives for the brethren.
I John 3:16**

West Texas Juniper
Height 28″

49

# STAND FAST

Paddling upstream in a lazy river can be done with little effort and minimal agitation of the surrounding waters. Yet as the downward flow increases in speed and intensity, our efforts must be stepped up and the agitation of the waters around us visibly and audibly becomes more apparent.

Since the garden of Eden, the enemy of our souls has been trying to convince humanity that we are more than just beings, created for God's pleasure. Let's face it, there is something inside of us that rebels at being *created* and we would prefer to believe that we are in control, or at least on the road to being there.

*"Ye shall not surely die: For God doth know that in the day ye eat thereof, then your eyes shall be opened, and ye shall be as gods, knowing good and evil"* (Genesis 3:4-5). This first course in self-realization and cosmic consciousness resulted in the very consequence God warned against, *death*. Each subsequent exercise of our *"divine"* wisdom has resulted in heartbreak and tragedy. Pick up a history book or a newspaper if you disagree. We are not designed to be gods; "me first" always bears bad fruit, and "me first" is the essence of the lie.

Years ago I had a pet roadrunner named Clark. I used to chuckle at the total abandonment he showed as he trotted around the pasture chasing dinner, courting his mate or investigating the buffet on my car grill. There was such an ease and peace possessed by this little character. Though his life was brief by our standards, I am sure he did not waste a second of it worrying about provision or regretting his past actions. He was able to enjoy each moment to the fullest. Why? because he had settled the issue of who he was (though I am sure it never entered his mind) and could enjoy being what he was created to be, a roadrunner.

Today the river of lies has stepped up its flow. New Age philosophies have painted mystical facades on the age-old lie recorded in Genesis, chapter three. It now requires more effort to go against the flow. The noise and agitation increase around the lives of those who stand fast in the truth. But like little ole Clark, I have found a peace in surrendering to the will of the Almighty God, and my feeble flesh no longer needs to bear the weight of responsibility that comes with being a "god." Nor does my soul have to subsist any longer on the bad fruit inevitably produced by such futile reasoning.

Genesis 3:1-7      Romans 5:8      Galatians 5:1

*Running to and fro*
*collecting what he needs.*
*Yet in the long run this we know,*
*from God's hand this runner feeds.*

*How much of this one's thoughts*
*are spent in efforts to succeed,*
*in trying **not** to worry*
*about the things that he will need?*

*Not many I assure you,*
*for he's content to be a bird.*
*To think he's more than just a creature*
*is a lie he's never heard.*

*He stands fast in his position,*
*a mere recipient of love,*
*a living way to glorify*
*God Almighty up above.*

*So stand fast in your position,*
*a simple creature dead in sin,*
*rejoicing God has made a way*
*for you to live again.*

***Stand fast therefore in the liberty wherewith Christ hath made us free . . .***
**Galatians 5:1**

West Texas Juniper

Height 19″

# LOVE BECOMES A PEOPLE

If you consider becoming involved with someone or a group, what do you watch for in that person or group? Does the way they treat people and each other affect your decision?

Have you ever heard or said a statement like this? "You Christians are always preaching about love and the right way, but all I ever see is a bunch of hypocrites who shun and condemn one another over whose way is *more right*. Thanks, but no thanks." Unfortunately, man's narrow attempts at self-righteousness seldom leave room for a differing opinion, and people do notice.

Sadly true, a loving Savior tries to reach out to a dying world through a body crippled by strife, self-righteousness and spiritual pride. Few people care to look past this grotesque figure into the eyes of the One within the body, and, tragically, they turn their backs on the One who died to save their souls.

All will certainly be held accountable. We Christians will have no excuse, for Scripture clearly teaches us to love one another. When we do follow His commands and love one another, that love shines bright and high above the rubble of this earth, drawing hungry souls to the Source.

We are all designed to respond to the love of God, by loving Him back. When we love those whom God loves, we show our love for Him.

***And be ye kind one to another, tenderhearted, forgiving one another, even as God for Christ's sake, hath forgiven you.*** **Ephesians 4:32**

I John 4:19     I John 5:2-3     I Thessalonians 4:9     Colossians 3:12-14

*We're the body of Christ.*
    *We pray for one another,*
*but how's the world to know*
    *unless we show we love our brother?*

*If asked to join a dog-fight*
    *would you step into the ring?*
*"Come help us fight our brother"*
    *is the song some Christians sing.*

*Since we're the Church of Christ,*
    *let love become our steeple;*
*'tis then the world can see*
    *a different kind of people.*

*A people who would suffer*
    *for reasons so unseen*
*with no "apparent" ends*
    *to justify their mean.*

*Folks, watch and then do wonder*
    *why these Christians act so odd,*
*as they're moved to watch more closely,*
    *hearts open up to God.*

*Salvation is not religion,*
    *salvation is from above,*
*given as "The Gift" to mankind*
    *who in turn reflect His love.*

*But as touching brotherly love ye need not that I write unto you:*
*for ye yourselves are taught of God to love one another.*
**I Thessalonians 4:9**

West Texas Juniper and Mesquite

Height 14″

# GOD'S WITHERED ROSE

I call this piece *God's Withered Rose* because I want the elderly to know that despite the often cruel and heartless treatment our society mandates the younger citizens should give to our seniors, the aged are still exceedingly precious in the eyes of God. They are still His, much loved, wept over, and tenderly held in His majestic hands. Why do we buy the lies that devalue the worth of the objects of God's love? What value system dare place comfort, convenience or time above a human soul? May I suggest a very devilish system is in operation in our hearts—a hellish factory of lies produced in a region of our hearts guarded viciously by pride, selfishness and a host of hell with their arsenal of apathy, greed and willful blindness.

If anger seems to leap out of this page, it is because I too am infected with this leaven, and it hurts to see my apathy evidenced through my actions. I desire a change, a solution to the lies that are eating away at mankind, killing the innocent at both ends of the spectrum of life.

I think we all know in our hearts the truth: God is no respecter of persons; the elderly are still our *neighbors*. We are commanded to *"love thy neighbor as thyself"* (Matthew 22:39). We have basic emotional needs in addition to the physical. For the elderly, the hearts' needs are unmet. You see, we all need to be valued, approved of and accepted, but these three needs we cannot meet by ourselves. They must come through others. Our society has conditioned us to be so busy seeking these blessings that we miss the avenue of truly receiving them: the giving of the same to others. The second reason for making this sculpture is, as you may have guessed, to exhort you to realize that there is not one emotional need we have that is not shared in equal intensity by those weathered pilgrims further down the path we walk. Ask the One who died for them how to let them know you see; then, more importantly, act and respond to their pleas for love.

James 1:21-27     Matthew 25:31-46

*I'm not a rose so withered*
*my heart can no more ache;*
*nor have I ceased to will to give,*
*though it's now my lot to take.*

*For time has done its number*
*on my old and dying shell,*
*but still inside this framework*
*is a person. Can't you tell?*

*A person who once laughed and played*
*in the sunshine of my youth,*
*loved and had a family,*
*raised them in the Truth.*

*The joys I shared in friendships,*
*the sorrows shared in loss,*
*I still desire to share again,*
*though that avenue seems lost.*

*I'm imprisoned—could you visit me?*
*Just let me know you see*
*that despite my feeble, dying frame,*
*it's still worthwhile to know me.*

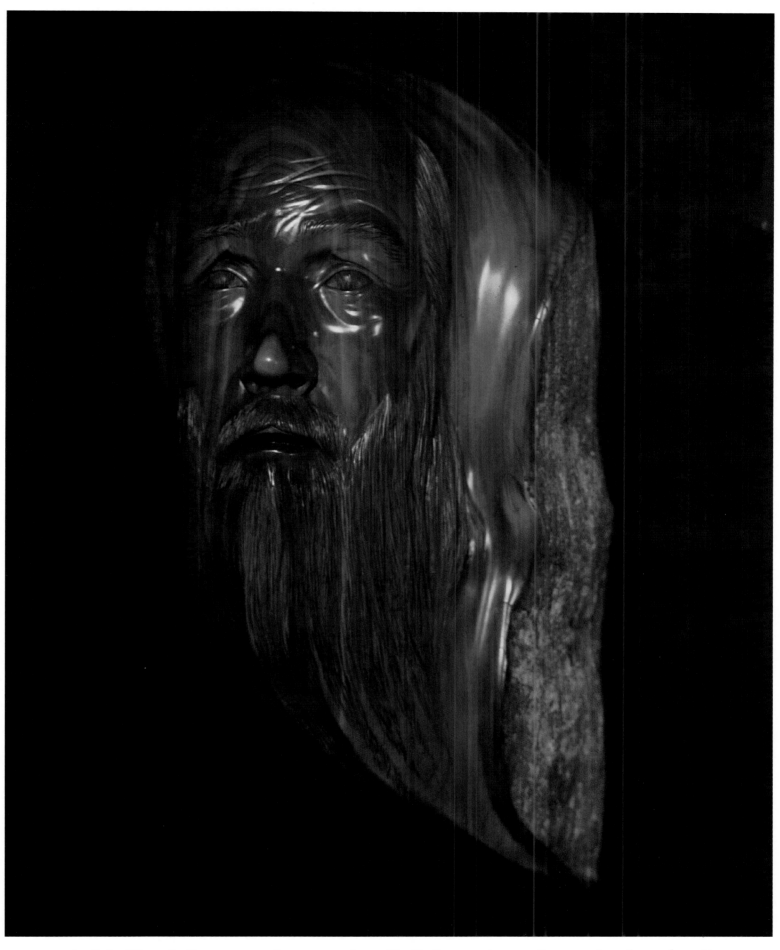

*And the King shall answer and say unto them, Verily I say unto you, Inasmuch ye have done it unto one of the least of these my brethren, ye have done it unto me.*
**Matthew 25:40**

West Texas Juniper
7/8 Life-Size

# VICTORY TUNE

Crosses. You see them around people's necks, on bumpers, over doorways, on buildings and on mountain tops—the symbol of a torture device from centuries past—a reminder of the fact that the One we Christians worship died a humiliating and painful death. The cross is a reminder of defeat. Man, if that is all there is to it, we are a morbid bunch of losers, aren't we? Well, praise God, that *is not all* there is to it. Death could not keep Jesus in the grave. Jesus broke death's perfect batting record and made a way for us to evade that *certain* fate.

The finality of the grave has always loomed over every life in every culture. Although we Americans are very adept at avoiding the issue, deep inside each soul is the dread of knowing we all face an unbeatable foe. We all will have one *final* breath.

We have heard it jokingly said, "There are only two things certain in life: death and taxes," but for those who truly take God at His word, the Author of life has chosen to grant a second chance at everlasting life. To do so, He had to defeat death. The battle took place on the cross where life conquered death. Therefore, the cross is a symbol of victory and a reminder of joy unspeakable. It is not a mere *memento mori*.

If the cross means nothing more to you than two sticks of wood, or if its true meaning has been reduced to a mere symbol of Christianity, here is an idea: Try sitting and genuinely thinking on the reality of death—yours. I do not like suggesting unpleasant tasks unless they have benefits that outweigh the pain involved. It is certainly my hope and prayer that anyone who takes that suggestion will ultimately find himself at the foot of the cross. May we humbly thank Jesus for the victory won there, and partake of the resurrection life He so graciously gives to those who believes.

I Corinthians 1:18-25       II Corinthians 15:17-21

*An empty cross,*
*    a risen King,*
*from death's dark womb*
*    new life does spring;*

*for though the cross*
*    did slay the Lamb,*
*death lost the fight*
*    to the great I AM.*

*That once foreboding*
*    fate that loomed,*
*was swallowed*
*    in a victory tune,*

*that Jesus sang,*
*    with angels fair*
*in that sweet Easter*
*    morning air,*

*"Come rise with Me*
*    and live anew;*
*receive My Word,*
*    for I AM true.*

*Rise high and free*
*    from death and sin;*
*repent, believe,*
*    be born again."*

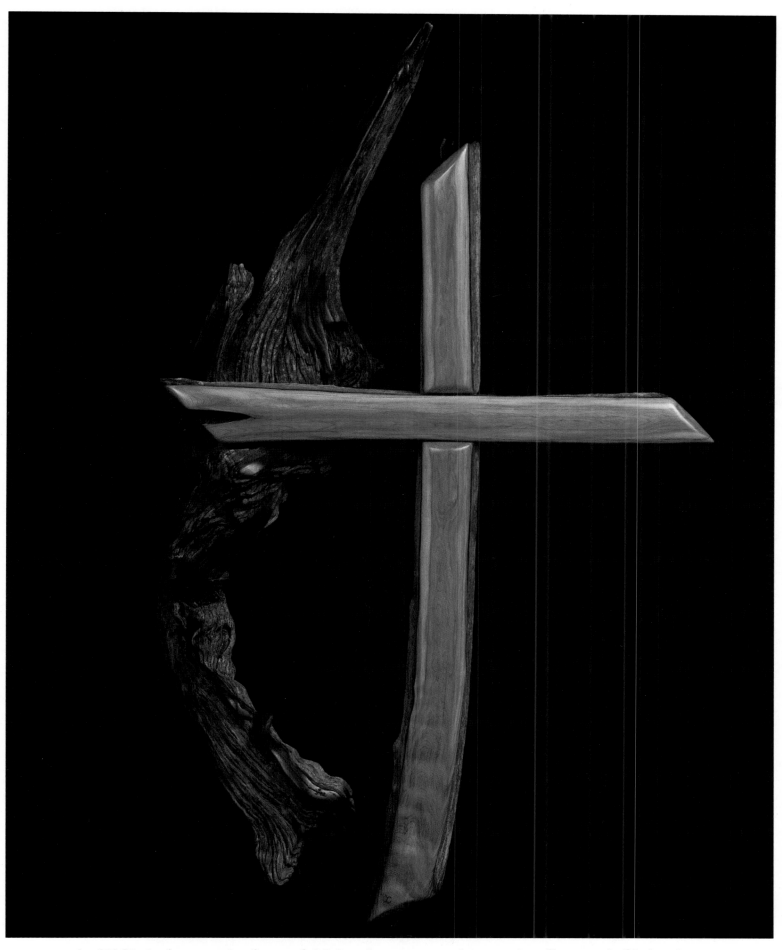

*And if Christ be not raised, your faith is vain; ye are yet in your sins. But now is Christ risen from the dead, and become the firstfruits of them that slept.*
**I Corinthians 15:17,20**

West Texas Juniper and Black Mesquite

Height 32″

# SET FREE

A familiar verse to many Christians, Isaiah 40:31 states: *"But they that wait upon the Lord shall renew their strength; they shall mount up with wings as eagles; they shall run, and not be weary; they shall walk, and not faint."* One evening as I sat on the edge of the canyon watching a golden eagle soar effortlessly in and out of the shadows, I was impressed by his freedom. He had no need to fear me for he was free to leave my presence, to ignore me, or to investigate the menace. Perhaps it was my singing, but he chose to gracefully split. *So be it, I was singing to Jesus anyway, you old . . . eagle.* I thought of the sculpture of an eagle I had begun and asked Jesus (His presence was very strong. He inhabits the praises of His people no matter how shabby the voice), *"Hey, isn't it about time we wrote the poem for that eagle sculpture?"*

As the breeze picked up, my heart was flooded with gratitude for the newly found freedom and my newly found friend. I no longer was a part of this dying old earth. My heart began to sing . . .

*Set free from the bonds*
*    of the earth's mighty grip*
*I fly now to Heaven*
*    and vow not slip,*

*for my eyes fix on Jesus*
*    the true King of kings,*
*my Lord and my Savior,*
*    my strength and my wings.*

*Flying through Heaven,*
*    though I live here on earth,*
*by accepting the promises,*
*    that come with rebirth;*

*like peace, joy and loving*
*    that flow through my heart,*
*health, strength and riches*
*    I've had from the start.*

*His arms are so laden*
*    with gifts He has given*
*to His children that reach*
*    towards their Father in Heaven.*

*Jesus is Truth,*
*    accept Him to be*
*your Lord and your Savior,*
*    then you'll be set free.*

***Then said Jesus to those Jews which believed on him, If ye continue in my word, then are ye
my disciples indeed; And ye shall know the truth, and the truth shall make you free.***
**John 8:31-32**

West Texas Juniper

31″ Wingspan

# DIAMONDS DIPPED IN CLAY

As a young adult, I saw the God I had learned of in the Bible as little more than the great cosmic kill-joy, with a few decent suggestions and too many unrealistic demands. *Flee fornication* seemed a bit too severe; *aside from a few obvious potential consequences, where was the harm?* If you get your thinking headed in a downward spiral, your deeds will soon be on its heels. Thus, step by step, sex was reduced to little more than an ever-diminishing physical thrill, and an ever-increasing source of those *not so few* obvious consequences.

I now see God's command as more than just a warning meant to save us untold grief. He has been cleansing and healing, and a jewel far more precious than I ever dreamed is beginning to emerge from the rubble of the past. He has shown me a glimpse of the gift's intended purpose. And what is its intended purpose, beyond the physical? Sex, as God designed it, is a vehicle of giving, of total commitment, of heartfelt love and desire—a means whereby a man and woman express: *You are my everything, and I give you my all.*

A double tragedy occurs in the mire of sexual sin. We not only cover the beautiful multifaceted surface of the jewel, but we also completely block the rich prismatic reflections of God's love shining brightly from within its depth.

**Flee from sexual immorality. All other sins a man commits are outside his body, but he who sins sexually sins against his own body. I Corinthians 6:18**

*I took a precious diamond*
*and dipped it in the clay,*
*knowing yet not knowing*
*I'd regret the act some day;*
*for alas the world has told me,*
*"this is all the jewel is for;*
*sure the clay looks dirty,*
*but you have to try the door."*

*Pleasure's for a season,*
*grief lasts on and on,*
*guilt mixed with delusion,*
*the purity is gone;*
*a jewel so bright and precious,*
*a priceless gift from God,*
*as the clay lay drying*
*became an earthen clod.*

*The value of a clump of soil*
*can be squandered in a thought,*
*and so I tossed the jewel around*
*its beauty I forgot;*
*'til light shone in my darkness,*
*death's lies began to fade;*
*the clay was chipped, a sparkle flew,*
*I saw the error I'd made.*

*I sought at once to cleanse the mess*
*my life had so become;*
*the Lord showed me the good, the bad,*
*the beauty from the scum.*
*At last the job neared completion*
*through a power not my own;*
*I wept at wasted years of dirt*
*as the diamond brightly shone.*

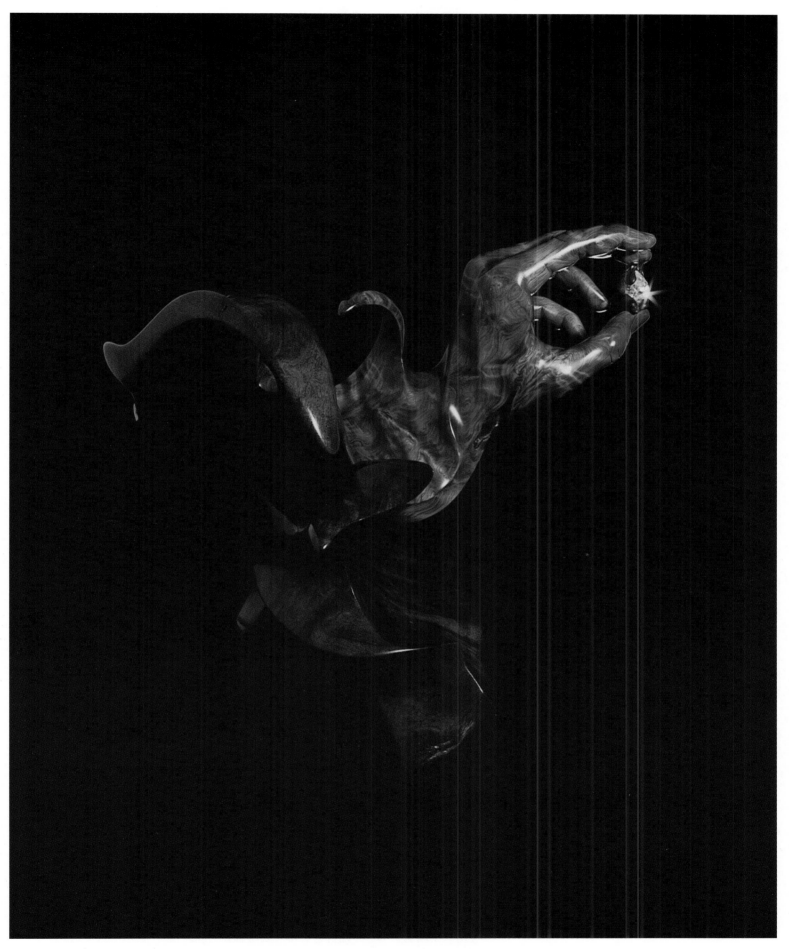

**And I will restore to you the years that the locust hath eaten, the cankerworm,
the caterpillar, and the palmerworm, my great army which I sent among you.
Joel 2:25**

West Texas Juniper and Mesquite

Height 10″ (Life-Size)

# THE TRUTH BEHIND THE MOVEMENT

In springtime, the words *wind* and *West Texas* are oftimes synonymous. Memories of street lights at noon, happy little children gleefully chasing tumbleweeds 'neath the red-brown sky, days of certain homeruns should the ball ever reach the batter, and effortless walks from school, as tons of rich Texas soil sailed past on its annual migration to Oklahoma.

I used to think of the wind as an entity—a not so benevolent being that took great pleasure in slamming skinny kids into playground equipment or hurling stinging sand at the legs of screaming school girls who frantically grabbed flapping jumpers and tugged at, alas, too short kneesocks.

But what if there were people who could see and befriend this creature?—who, instead of being dribbled across the playground, could grab his hands and be pulled in a game of crack the whip or be swung around as with a playful uncle? Even by imitating their motions could we experience the same thing as those who know? Maybe Nicodemus was a skinny kid once and so understood well the analogy Jesus gave concerning those who are born of the Spirit.

As with Nicodemus, we were formerly *pushed* by the demands of the law. Yet upon being born again, our *desires* are changed and we are *led* by His Spirit.

***But the natural man receiveth not the things of the Spirit of God: for they are foolishness unto him: neither can he know them, because they are spiritually discerned.*
I Corinthians 2:14**

John 3:1-7

I Corinthians 2: 9-16

*Born of the Spirit
   we follow the wind
invisible captain
   of those born again,*

*but others can't see
   the commands that are given,
they follow the dust
   as by the wind it is driven.*

*They look as the wind
   blows through the trees,
and say, "we'll make motions
   like unto these."*

*Oh, if they could see
   the hands of the wind
caress and cajole
   the dry leaf to spin,*

*instead of believing
   the wind pushes to send,
they'd see trees wildly dancing
   in the arms of a friend.*

*And who has known
   the mind of a breeze,
surely not those
   who are watching the trees.*

*The wind bloweth where it listeth, and thou hearest the sound thereof, but canst not tell whence it cometh, and whither it goeth: so is every one that is born of the Spirit.*
**John 3:8**

West Texas Juniper on Walnut
Height 34″ Length 64″

# PROBLEM MATH

Look upon a loved one. Is it the person you really see, or merely the light reflected from him? You can capture that light image on film, but the true person escapes and moves on through time. You are left with but a memory. The light reveals (glorifies) the person to your eyes, but the light and the person are separate.

Jesus said, *"... He that hath seen me hath seen the Father..."* (John 14:9) Are they therefore the same person? Jesus spoke of Himself as being the light of the world, but the Holy Spirit seems to be doing the work of light in that His job is to glorify the Son.

At about this point in the discussion, my *mind* begins to lose its grip on trying to explain the Trinity. One God ... three persons ... all one. This is an apparent contradiction, but an impossible gospel if it is not totally true. So what's a body to do?

*"Through faith we understand..."* (Hebrews 11:3) When I have one hand full of scriptures saying God is one, and one hand full of scriptures saying God is three, I have "an issue" in hand. So, drop the issue, focus the eyes on Jesus—the Author and Finisher of our faith—and simply accept in faith that both are true. Trust and seek understanding, not an explanation. If we, in childlike faith, take God at His word and allow our questions to draw us into prayer (relating to God), then we'll have a clear focus on what is truly important. Our goal is to know God in all His holiness, not simply to know about Him. The latter comes through the former, not the reverse.

This sculpture depicts the Trinity. The Father is indicated by the light bursting forth from the center, and Jesus, the King of kings, is seen with His crown. The crown also makes up the tail of the dove and His head is made up of Christ's beard. All individual, yet one.

God clearly states, there are three
   that bear witness up in Heaven;
the Father, the Word and the Holy Ghost,
   this spells three now, not eleven.
Just as clearly it is stated
   these three are truly one;
by all of my mathematics
   I can't see how this is done.

My calculations tell me
   to choose between the two;
one theory must be false
   the other theory true.
If I believe they are just one,
   I deny redemption's plan,
I say no one was truly sent
   to die for the sins of man.

So they really must be three,
   but God can only number one;
so this saying they are separate
   denies the deity of the Son.
Earthly wisdom doesn't count
   when it comes to the ways of Heaven.
I can remember back, when I was a child,
   I couldn't even count to seven.

*So what makes me so different now?*

**For God, who commanded light to shine out of darkness, hath shined into our hearts,
to give the light of the knowledge of the glory of God in the face of Jesus Christ.
II Corinthians 4:6**

West Texas Juniper

Height 26″ Width 42″

# GYPSY DOLPHINS

God states very clearly in His Word that we should work. He would not frustrate us by giving us a command without also supplying a job that enables us to fulfill that command. But we have this pitiful tendency to take our eyes off the Source and put them on the circumstances. In fact, we humans are the only inhabitants of this planet that have mastered the *art* of worrying.

Jesus, in the gospels, tells us how His Father cares for the sparrows and ravens and then asks: *"Are ye not much better than they?"* (Matthew 6:26) He speaks of the lilies of the field that neither toil nor spin, yet are clothed more splendidly than a king, and asks: *"Wherefore, if God so clothe the grass of the field . . . shall he not much more clothe you, O ye of little faith?"* (Matthew 6:30) It all comes down to believing God or not; *"for our heavenly Father knoweth that ye have need of all these things"* (Matthew 6:32).

Is our belief to be a passive: *Here I am, God. Feed me and clothe me?* No, He gives us a definite command of action, which is followed by the supplying of our daily bread: *"Seek ye first the kingdom of God, and his righteousness; and all these things shall be added unto you"* (Matthew 6:33). How do the sparrows seek the Kingdom of God? They do what they were created to do, glorify God. We too must fulfill our purpose, because *"everyone who is called by my name . . . I created for my glory . . ."* (Isaiah 43:7)

Through sin we lose the ability to communicate with God and do His will; through the righteousness imputed to us by Jesus Christ, *"we have peace with God"* (Romans 5:1) and the power of the resurrection, which helps us do what we are called to do. As we go about the tasks He has given us to do, He takes care of the rest.

Psalms 19:1     Revelation 4:11     Matthew 6:19-34

*Gypsy dolphins*
  *running free,*
*possessing naught*
  *they own the sea;*
*for though they hold*
  *no title deed,*
*they've food and shelter*
  *all they need.*
*Still they must look*
  *unto their guide*
*who shows them where*
  *sweet morsels hide,*
*instead of wondering*
  *if there'll be*
*sufficient fish*
  *in next week's sea.*
*Our Lord said we*
  *should emulate*
*this simple trusting,*
  *childlike trait*
*of believing that*
  *His word is true,*
*and seeking but*
  *His will to do.*

***Be careful for nothing; but in every thing by prayer and supplication with thanksgiving
let your requests be made known unto God.***
**Philippians 4:6**

West Texas Juniper on Mesquite

Height 8″ Length 15″

# DETERMINED

I do not know if you have ever been thoroughly disgusted with yourself, but if that leads you to cry out to God for help, then it is a good thing. The apostle Paul when writing to the Christians in Corinth stated, *"But we all, with open face beholding as in a glass the glory of the Lord, are changed into the same image from glory to glory, even as by the Spirit of the Lord"* (II Corinthians 3:18).

If we have a heart that is willing to be changed, God will bring us to a place where it will be changed in a beautiful way; but the road to that place is often painful and ugly. In a variety of ways He leads us to a vantage point where we can gaze across the expanses of our hearts and view the gray landscape scarred by selfishness, bitterness, lust and greed and shrouded in an acrid mist of pride. Yet from every vantage point there remains a facade of self-righteousness that will convince even keen eyes that *I am not that bad*. The only weapon that will lift this veil is faith; if God says my heart is desperately wicked and deceitful, then, *it is*, regardless of what I *prefer* to believe. Crash, down comes the facade and we understand the reality of our sinfulness. Our response should be as one of the many uttered by sinners and recorded on the pages of the Bible. *"Have mercy on me, O God, according to thy lovingkindness: according to the multitude of thy tender mercies blot out my transgressions. Wash me throughly from mine iniquity, and cleanse me from my sin"* (Psalms 51:1-2). In other words, help God, I need a savior. I cannot make it alone. As good as the apostle Paul was, he wrote these words in the book of Romans, *"For I know in me (that is, in my flesh,) dwelleth no good thing: for to will is present with me; but how to perform that which is good I find not"* (Romans 7:18). Paul was at the vantage point of humility; viewing his wicked heart, he subsequently cried out *"O wretched man that I am! who shall deliver me from the body of this death?"* (Romans 7:24) He goes on to give the answer to his plea for help, *"I thank God through Jesus Christ our Lord"* (Romans 7:25). Jesus will come to our rescue. How? Again, through faith in His promises. He promised throughout the entire counsel and history of the Bible to send us a savior from our sins. He also illustrated it in innumerable ways in the Old Testament. God promises to save us and He cannot lie; so He will! Rest in His promises. I do not have room to even begin to list them, but only Jesus can and only Jesus will free us from the bondage of sin. The promises are there; learn them and establish them in your heart *daily* as truth. The lies of feelings, circumstances and the pressures of the world to conform to its standards do not hit us for just one hour a week, so how can we expect an hour of truth on Sunday to even begin to combat the lies. Unless your mind is a total vacuum it is filled with something! The choice of what to put in is yours, as are the consequences of your decision.

Imagine a falcon flying in the air; the air represents the word of God. The warm currents of His promises lift the falcon high above danger and onto glorious things; but to fly, the falcon must push his wings into the air and exercise faith, so to speak. In a very determined manner he must maintain the wind under his wings. That foundation enables him to do the awe inspiring aerobatics of the fastest bird on earth, and that sure beats being firewood.

Psalms 32, 38 and 58      Jeremiah 17:9      Romans 7:14-8:3      I Corinthians 3:14-18

*I so want to escape*
*what keeps pulling me down,*
*to be free from corruption*
*and this life on the ground.*

*So I try and I try*
*to do what is right,*
*but a part of my makeup*
*aborts every flight.*

*What is the answer,*
*where is the clue*
*that will help me escape*
*and fly faithful and true?*

*The answer is so simple*
*it escapes my searching eye;*
*Christ Jesus came to lift me up*
*for He knew I couldn't fly.*

*Rest your wings upon My promises,*
*let them lift you to a place*
*where your heart will change*
*in the glory of looking on My face.*

*Determine what I said is true*
*despite all circumstance and fear;*
*your part is true believing,*
*My part to bring you near.*

*Whereby are given unto us exceeding great and precious promises: that by these ye might be partakers of the divine nature, having escaped the corruption that is in the world through lust. And beside this giving all diligence, add to your faith . . .*
**II Peter 1:4-5**

West Texas Juniper

Height 23″

# INNOCENT BLOOD

*Captive, betrayed, unable to flee or cry for help, she struggles while a determined foe begins the torture that ends in death and a mass unmarked grave.* Adolf Hitler instituted laws which, step by step, eventually resulted in the premeditated deaths of millions of innocent lives. The scene above was repeated thousands of times *before* the subsequent steps ever took a life outside a mother's womb. A blind man never sees the obvious; fools busy professing their wisdom are just as unlikely to see the pit at the end of their road. What happened to the highly educated intellects of Germany? It seems they had a problem, but were not intelligent enough to produce a solution that didn't contain murder and their own eventual ruin. The *wise* of today say God's standards and morality are foolish and not pertinent to today's problems. Pertinent or not, God's law, if followed, would solve today's problems. But our *wise* men devise their own answers to the vexations of today's society (i.e. over-population): *Why, simply chop the little babies in pieces.* I tell those dear fools, they have devised no new thing, but merely borrowed from Adolf Hitler. History credits him with an awful atrocity and a warning to those who would follow his logic. People, you must take heed, lest the axe you raise to justify your sin today, fall back upon your hoary heads tomorrow. Christians, when our vote remains silent, it is cast for the opposition. The Lord gives us a scripture that tells us to speak up against this senseless slaughter.

*Open your mouth for the dumb, [those unable to speak for themselves], for the rights of all who are left desolate and defenseless.* **Proverbs 31:8, AB**

*Professing themselves to be wise, they became as fools.* **Romans 1:22**

*See the beauty and innocence of a child in the dove,*
*    gentleness, laughter, giving of love.*
*Both helpless and harmless they live and are born,*
*    mating for life, at death they do mourn.*

*In robbing a nest no one calls it a lie*
*    that as the egg breaks a fledgling does die.*
*So tell me this riddle and study it well,*
*    for a hideous truth the answer will tell.*

*If an egg holds a fledgling, a young living dove,*
*    what holds laughter and the giving of love?*
*In breaking an egg we know that we kill;*
*    so why isn't it murder when a child's heart*
*is made still?*

A question to test the consistency of one's logic:

In order to obtain a coat made from the skins of unborn giant pandas, would one have to kill pandas?

Regardless of your answer, if one were to make a large coat of the skins of unborn panda, there would soon be no pandas left and no reason to ponder the question.

*The wicked is snared in the work of his own hands.*
**Psalms 9:16**

West Texas Juniper on Mesquite

Height 10″

# CONVINCING POSE

There is just one truth I want to get across with this poem and sculpture, but it needs a little illustration, beginning with this touch of background.

Being raised in a very flat terrain, I was 17 years of age before I ever ran down a hill much over thirty feet in altitude. Consequently I had never tried to stop myself when running down a hill.

That is the background. This is a story of gravity and gratitude.

On an early morning jaunt to a beach near San Francisco, I found myself thrilling to the experience of running down a long steep hill. The dense fog was exhilarating so I poured on the speed. Suddenly, our guide to this secluded beach began yelling at me to stop. I was so intrigued by the fact that my legs seemed powerless to slow down, that I did not really notice the panic in his cries. I just kept running. Suddenly, I was tackled by a very angry acquaintance, who immediately began to yell insults aimed at my intelligence (or lack there of). My agitation over this guy's attitude and actions suddenly changed to overwhelming gratitude, as I heard the distant crash of waves on rocks at the base of the cliff, which lay just a few yards ahead. I was not at all grateful for the way he chose to stop me until I realized what he had saved me from.

Until the reality of sin and its certain consequences of misery and eternal death really become a reality to us, we do not truly appreciate the salvation Jesus provides for us. The greater the sin, the greater the love that forgives that sin. The apostle Paul knew the reality of both the love and the wrath of God. The fact that he called himself "chief of sinners" probably accounted for the tremendous love that caused him to brave multiple beatings, privation, imprisonment and, ultimately, death in an effort to share the news of Jesus' saving grace with the multitudes he saw running their certain course into the jaws of death. *"The love of God constraineth us . . ."* (II Corinthians 5:14)

Paul maintained a certain attitude that caused his life to convince men of the reality of God's judgement seat and the love that saves us from the certain consequences of our sin. He was like the one Jesus spoke of in Luke, chapter 7: *"Her sins, which are many, are forgiven; for she loved much . . ."* (Luke 7:47) Paul never cheated himself out of the revelation of the expanse of the love of God by fearing to allow God to show him the depth of his sinfulness. If we would grow in the knowledge of the love of God as revealed in the shed blood of Jesus, we must allow Him to show us just what it covers.

Luke 7:36-50      II Corinthians 5:14

*A myriad of angles*
*  are there at our command,*
*almost all in which we fall,*
*  only one in which we stand.*

*Infinite directions, moves*
*  that we can make,*
*and many different roads of thought*
*  our roving hearts can take.*

*Some are good or better,*
*  others hard and cruel;*
*but which the thought of victory's way*
*  that can both guide and rule?*

*The constraining love of God*
*  convincing of the fact*
*that though He loves us, God shall judge*
*  our each and every act*

*Is the truth, if weighed in balance*
*  of His mercy and His wrath,*
*that will define a love, within whose hands,*
*  is the straight and narrow path.*

***For the love of God constraineth us . . .***
**II Corinthians 5:14**

West Texas Juniper
Height 9″

73

# UNDER THE SHADOW OF HIS WING

*NO! You're wrong, aren't you? You can't be serious? Not him, oh God, not him.* The news broke over me like waves. First overwhelmingly real, then surely a mistake, then deeper and deeper the unwelcomed message drove into my heart and grew until it became an unmistakable reality. A man I loved and admired, my pastor, was gone—taken home in a plane crash. Then as shock turned into pain and sorrow, questions began to arise, *Why Father . . . why him? . . . why so young? . . . why?* God answered in a gentle command: *Pray. Pray that I may be glorified—glorified to his family and friends as the God of all comfort. Thank Me for turning this time of sorrow into something powerfully good. I am able. Trust Me and pray. Don't ask why, but pray.*

The response wasn't the answer I wanted. But as I obeyed, a soothing ointment was spread on my heart. The hurting subsided, and tears of sorrow made way for tears of rejoicing as I shared in Pastor's joy.

He was finally home with his *Father Dear*, and his family was experiencing a revelation of God that could come no other way than through the desperate need of a breaking heart. I knew this faithful Friend was there to comfort and console, for through the smaller avenue of my own loss and hurt, a gentle sweetness directed my eyes to One who truly understood my pain.

*Under the shadow of His wing*
*a channel of grace is open,*
*for if our joy were full*
*we'd have no cause for hoping.*

*For grace must have a channel,*
*a vent to come within,*
*a heart that's torn and bleeding*
*to make it whole again.*

*And as this action happens,*
*a side of God we see*
*as soft as any feather,*
*so real and strong is He.*

*His thoughts toward us are many,*
*His delight is to reveal*
*His ability to comfort,*
*His ability to heal.*

*So stand beneath His shadow,*
*in hope, lift high your head.*
*You'll see His wing above you,*
*there's One died in your stead.*

*To reveal these words so truthful,*
*without clouds there is no rain;*
*so too His kiss of comfort*
*cannot come except through pain.*

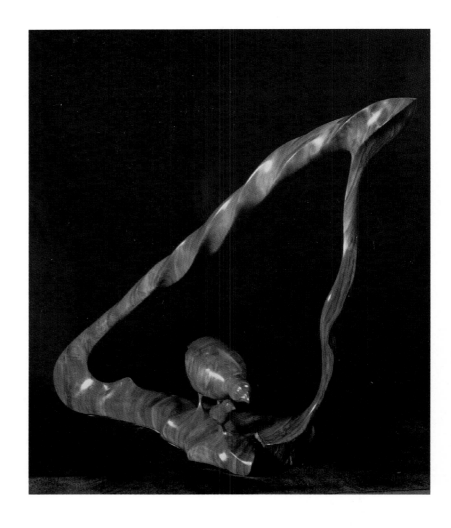

**Blessed be God, even the Father of our Lord Jesus Christ, the Father of mercies, and the God of all comfort; Who comforteth us in all our tribulation . . . as ye are partakers of the sufferings, so shall ye be also of the consolation.**
**II Corinthians 1:3-7**

West Texas Juniper

Height 18″

# CARDINAL RULE

*. . . to give unto them beauty for ashes, the oil of joy for mourning, the garment of praise for the spirit of heaviness; that they might be called trees of righteousness, the planted of the Lord, that he might be glorified.* **Isaiah 61:3**

When you in faith pray *God be glorified,* expect to see it. I doubt we'll ever be able to out-guess God about *how* He will be glorified, but He will be revealed and understood, you can stand on it.

The previous poem speaks of God's ability to comfort; this one speaks of a means of comfort He used. My pastor was the only one taken in that mountain plane crash. The three survivors, though all very critically injured, spoke of the crash as they gained strength on their road to full recovery. What moved me the most was their account of Pastor's praying for them as the plane lost altitude. Prayer is conversation with God. When the plane and his body were shattered, this godly man instantly stood before his Lord and God, his conversation uninterrupted. How can I know such a thing?

There was no mistaking the fact, this man knew Jesus intimately. To know Jesus is eternal life, whether in the body or out of the body. We are spirits; if we through our spirits know Jesus, that relationship will not be destroyed by the destruction of our "earth-suit." *The fear of death is displaced by the knowing of the author of life.* I know that some day my body will go back to the earth; but just as surely, I know that my Redeemer lives, and by this I live.

*And this is life eternal, that they might know thee the only true God, and Jesus Christ, whom thou hast sent.* **John 17:3**

*My life is but a vapour*
*I live it day to day*
*never knowing when the wind*
*will blow it fast away.*

*By knowing God, through His Son,*
*eternal life I hold,*
*and knowing Him won't pass away*
*when my limbs grow stiff and cold.*

*For what is your life? It is even a vapour, that appeareth for a little time
and then vanisheth away.*
**James 4:14**

West Texas Juniper on Huisache

Height 15"

# THE PURPOSE OF THE WINGS

Does God lament? Does He cry out with an aching voice over the loss we choose to suffer? Of course He does. We hear the echo of a Father's heartache ringing throughout the Scriptures, *"To day, if ye will hear his voice, harden not your hearts, as in provocation in the day of temptation in the wilderness"* (Hebrews 3:7-8).

If anyone ever missed the point, it would have to be the children of Israel as they marched through the wilderness. God delivered an entire nation from slavery. What they saw and experienced—the plagues of Egypt, the parting of the Red Sea, a pillar of fire and smoke to guide them, manna each day, water springs in the desert, and the Shekinah glory of Almighty God descending daily upon the tabernacle—was a tremendous display of God's works, yet their response was one of selfish ingratitude. Basically, translated into today's language, it was, *But what do I get out of this deal?* In addition to deliverance from slavery, daily provision of strength, food, water, health, clothing and the assurance of His divine presence and guidance, in addition to the obvious, they were given the opportunity to know this wonderful God.

God said to Moses: *"Tell the children of Israel; Ye have seen what I did unto the Egyptians and how I bare you on eagles' wings, and brought you unto myself"* (Exodus 19:4). The point of bringing them out of slavery was to bring them into a relationship with God Himself.

We, at times, are no different. Jesus came, displayed His tremendous love, delivered us from the slavery of sin and provided us with *"all things that pertain unto life and godliness"* (II Peter 1:3), and still we fail to take our eyes off ourselves long enough to see our wonderful Creator and Savior. We too ignore the tremendous privilege of actually knowing this incredible, omnipotent God. If ever anyone ever missed the point . . .

Exodus 19:4     I Corinthians 5:14-15

*Out of the flames of affliction*
  *I brought you a great length;*
*I bare you upon eagles' wings*
  *over trials beyond your strength.*

*I did it for one reason,*
  *to bring you unto Me.*
*Your eyes look on My promises,*
  *but their fulfillment you can't see.*

*Your heart longs for the meager crumbs*
  *of a kingdom cold and dark,*
*and cannot see the banquet*
  *prepared inside My heart.*

*Communion with the most High God,*
  *true abandon in His love,*
*is the feast the Lamb provided*
  *when He shed for us His blood*

*and allowed us to come unto Him,*
  *the purpose of the wings*
*He supplies through revelation*
  *and the joy repentance brings.*

***Ye have seen what I did unto the Egyptians, and how I bare you on eagles' wings,
and brought you unto myself.***
**Exodus 19:4**

West Texas Juniper and Black Mesquite

Height 8″  Wingspan 6 1/2″

# CURRENTS OF CIRCUMSTANCES

Here comes life, fast and furious, right at you, whoosh. Seems you are still reeling from one blow and dodging the next when something sneaks up from your blind side to topple you into despair. The pace of life today leaves little room for recuperation before the urgent pushes us into the next scene. When I do take the time to reflect, my mind is often filled with that enormous little three letter question, W-H-Y ? I have seen so many people, myself included, who have held so tightly to the right to know what is going on that they have missed the answer all together. We need to let go of the *right* to know in order to grasp the answer.

This next thought, though simple, contains a powerful answer to the dilemma of swirling circumstances. The book of Hebrews views the race of life and gives this advice: *"For consider Him who has endured such hostility by sinners against Himself, so that you may not grow weary and lose heart"* (Hebrews 12:3 NAS). Stop considering the circumstances or potential problems and take the time to carefully regard the person of Jesus Christ, who He really is and what He has really done for us. If we truly know Jesus to be an all-wise and good God, His selfless love for us displayed on the cross should convince us that the circumstances He sends our way are working together for good, even when our limited vision cannot see Christ's character being revealed in and to us.

Let's face it. In the times when, through prayer, we focus clearly on Jesus, we begin to sense His presence, realize His goodness, and finally trust in His faithfulness. *"Thou wilt keep him in perfect peace whose mind is stayed on thee; because he trusteth in thee"* (Isaiah 26:3). I said it was simple, not easy. It is much easier for us to focus on the circumstances and their boasts of more to come, than to use eyes of faith to see our sovereign Lord guiding us firmly through the storms of life.

Psalms 91    Isaiah 26:3    Romans 8:28    Hebrews 12:3    I John 3:16

*It seems the flow of my environment*
   *is spinning me around;*
*surging floods of circumstances*
   *knock my feet off solid ground.*
*As much as I desire it,*
   *outside these waters I can't thrive,*
*for there is Someone in these waters*
   *aptly keeping me alive.*

*If in the trials and tribulations*
   *I could in trust discern*
*the goodness of the all-wise God,*
   *I might welcome every turn*
*that wrenches from my grasp*
   *things I hold so very dear*
*in exchange for explanations,*
   *I admit, seem quite unclear.*

*But faith in Him who justifies*
   *the ungodly through His blood,*
*can set me firm upon the rock,*
   *sustain me through the flood.*
*For He is here amid the waters,*
   *revealing with each tide,*
*a faithful, Holy Lord of all*
   *standing at my side.*

*For consider Him who has endured such hostility by sinners against Himself,*
*so that you may not grow weary and lose heart.*
**Hebrews 12:3 NAS**

West Texas Juniper on Black Walnut

Height 15″

# GENTLE POWER

When we are learning something like a trade, there are certain levels of achievement that we can reach without having a very clear grasp on the working of the tools or the structures. These levels, however, are not too high and are slow in coming. If we take the time to familiarize ourselves with the tools and their functions, limits and proper use, we will be better equipped for the job. A good firm relationship with the teacher and a clear ability to understand him, or her, makes a better student as well. All the instruction in the world is a waste on a person void of understanding. When a teacher gives a student a fifteen minute break, he has to retrain him. Right? Believe me, because I'm a teacher. Although a student may be able to repeat a step, if he doesn't *grasp* what he's doing, he won't go very far before the teacher has to push him again. Like a rock being pushed uphill, eventually he will roll back over the teacher's foot, which is very frustrating for both the teacher and the rock.

Do you reckon this might be the reason the Holy Spirit, through Paul, wrote the prayers found in Ephesians, chapters one and three, and Colossians, chapter one? They contain important lessons for the first century Christians. In all three prayers there are pleas for the Church to be blessed with understanding. Understanding of what? Of the power that is available to change us from within, the power working in us to free us from our sin—an understanding of the inheritance we have as children of God and brothers and sisters of Jesus. Paul wants us to have a grasp (experientially) of the vast, all-encompassing love of God. God desires to give us an understanding of His will for us: wisdom, thankfulness, joy and patience, as well as the knowledge how better to use these tools so we may come to know Him and thus further the kingdom of God. The main thing God desires to give us is an understanding of Himself. The tools are there to help us find Him so that we may discover Him in all His fulness.

The best analogy I can think to give you right now is this: I could *see,* in my mind's eye, a dove within the old dead tree I found lying on the canyon ledge. I had tools, skills and talents available to me to aid in the task of *realizing* this dove. But each stroke of the knife or rasp had one goal or purpose behind it, which was to *discover* the dove. I was working towards something much more tangible than the image in my mind. Everything I did had that one goal and purpose; each time I picked up a tool it was to further that purpose, to achieve the goal.

Let me try to tie all this together. We have an incredible array of tools at our disposal, purchased for us at Calvary. Through faith we step into this inheritance. We are given an incredible instructor, the Holy Spirit. His working within us is the talent, the ability. He also imprints upon our hearts and minds the image of God, in Jesus, thus making clear in our hearts the goal, which is daily to know and more clearly realize Jesus Christ, our Creator and Lord. If we begin to chip away at the tree of life slowly and without the purpose of knowing Jesus, our task is slow and grievous, and the best of tools are of little value. With our purpose established (as Paul expressed in Philippians 3:7-16), let us work side by side with the instructor—using the tools He provides, being aided by an understanding of our *goal* and offering a willing, obedient heart. Therein is a joy unspeakable that is full of glory.

Ephesians 1:15-23     Ephesians 3:14-21     Colossians 1:9-19

*There's a person working in my heart*
*beyond my mortal strength,*
*a power without measure*
*that knows no bounds nor length;*
*a power that raised from the dead*
*a man that sin had slain,*
*and daily strengthens mightily*
*the soul that's born again.*

*O help me know the power*
*that's strengthening my soul;*
*give me eyes to understand the gift*
*You've sent to make me whole.*
*Grant me hunger, Lord, for the things*
*that please You, God Most High,*
*and through realization of Your love,*
*help my flesh to daily die.*

*My Guide, Sweet Holy Spirit,*
*point me always to the Son.*
*For with eyes fixed on His person,*
*God's will in me is done;*
*and though it come upon me daily,*
*help me not believe the lie*
*that would have me to look inward*
*on my own strength to rely.*

**That He would grant you, according to the riches of his glory,**
**to be strengthened with might by his Spirit in the inner man.**
**Ephesians 3:16**

West Texas Juniper on Mesquite
Height 18″  Wingspan 14″

# STAND UP

In Central Mexico, dogs, if you go by appearance only, are seemingly bred to produce disgusting, scroungy, desperately nasty looking beasts. All association with these potentially rabid mongrels should be avoided, if given a choice! I developed this slanted opinion of our canine neighbors to the south through several unpleasant "small group discussions" with these mangy brutes. From the experiences, I learned two important lessons: one, if you run, you will most certainly be pursued; two, if you take an offensive stance, arm yourself and move into the pack, you will clearly see the yellow streaks running up their fleeing backsides. You see, most dogs speak "rock" fluently, but you must address them in no uncertain terms.

The point I'm making from my slightly exaggerated slander of *man's best friend* is this: defensive words, actions and posture are blatant, discrediting statements of doubt and fear. If you declare, "Jesus is the victorious Risen Lord of all," in an apologetic mumble, is it any wonder people reject your words? Come on, it doesn't work that way!

We are commanded to preach the gospel to all the world. Preaching is proclaiming the truth as THE TRUTH; anything short of that, and you are not preaching!!!

Rest assured, when you take a stand for Jesus, the hounds of hell will bay and lunge for the throat; but God will fight the battle as you, *"having done all, stand"* (Ephesians 6:13) in faith. The devil will flee for *IT IS WRITTEN!*

**Note:** This message and poem have very little to do with this sculpture of a largemouth bass: on second thought maybe they do.

**Note:** Since so many people have asked if this is the natural grain of the wood, I feel a need to say: yes it is. On very, very rare occasions, juniper will have a curly grain. I got eleven sculptures from this one tree; I'm still looking for another one.

*Move a mountain*
*    take a stand,*
*don't fall prey*
*    to fear's demand;*
*for though the world*
*    stands posed to kill,*
*stand firm in God*
*    His Truth prevails.*
*Should you protect*
*    the gospel's claims?*
*Did Jesus say,*
*    "defend my Name"?*
*Or is our task*
*    His mouth to be,*
**proclaiming***, "He*
*    has set men free."*
*Defensive posture*
*    says to all,*
*"this man fears*
*    his cause will fall."*
*Destruction comes*
*    as no surprise*
*to those who walk*
*    in compromise.*

*Your silent vote,*
*    your coward's cry,*
*screams loudly that*
*    your life's a lie.*

*Where is the wise? where is the scribe? where is the disputer of this world? hath not God made foolish*
*the wisdom of this world? For after that in the wisdom of God the world by wisdom knew*
*not God, it pleased God by the foolishness of preaching to save them that believe.*
**I Corinthians 1:20-21**

West Texas Juniper on Mesquite

Length 13″

# NO RAGGED CAPE

One essential to salvation is the God-given realization that we are sinners, totally separated from God, hopelessly unable to do anything of our own to regain right-standing with the God who created us and against whom we have rebelled. Total reliance on the finished work of Jesus on Calvary and His resurrection from the dead to cover our sins and give us the power to live the life God created us to live is also an essential in *maintaining* a victorious Christian walk.

So often we slip into the sin of unbelief, trying to *be worthy* or combat sin through our own ragged efforts. Paul wrote to the Galatians, *"Received ye the Spirit by the works of the law, or by the hearing of faith? Are ye so foolish? Having begun in the Spirit, are ye now made perfect by the flesh?"* (Galatians 3:23) Charles Finney commented on the same subject, and pointed out an inherent by-product of sin: "No work of the law has any tendency whatsoever to combat sin, but rather establishes the soul in self-righteousness." The writer of the letter to the Hebrews gives the God-given battle plan against this root of all sins: *"Looking unto Jesus the author and finisher of our faith..."* (Hebrews 12:2) Faith in Jesus—His character, His abilities and His faithfulness to fulfill the promises in His Word—is, according to First John 5:4, *"the victory that overcometh the world."* What is gained through the victory? The revelation of the love of God and the subsequent power to love Him back.

We are not designed to obey mere rules, codes or formulas, but rather the Person who gives them, for in Him alone is the sole source of the power to obey the law. The law is summed up in these two commands: *"Thou shalt love the Lord thy God with all thy heart, and with all thy soul, and with all thy strength and with all thy mind; and thy neighbour as thyself"* (Luke 10:27). Just as a mirror cannot manufacture light, so too we cannot produce the love we are commanded to give God. Upon the revelation of the love He gives us, our design is to reflect, freely give back His love; this is done by following His commands as an act of love toward the One who loved us first, and should require no more sacrifice and effort than it takes a mirror to reflect an image. Our efforts should rather be spent focusing on the Source of light in thanksgiving, praise and worship. By *"looking unto Jesus the author and finisher of our faith..."* our actions will spring out of a deep desire to please, rather than a begrudging *I suppose I must* attitude. To a God who looks on the intention and motives of the heart, the difference is as day and night.

If we walk in unbelief, whatever form it takes: rebellion, self-righteousness, pride, striving to be worthy, or simply believing circumstances over God's promises and failing to act, we then are shaded from the revelation of His love and have little to give, reflect, save our own ragged darkness.

*... and all our righteousnesses are as filthy rags ...* Isaiah 64:6

*Filthy rags*
   *upon the back*
*the more you have*
   *the more you lack,*

*for try your best*
   *to cleanse the soul,*
*self-righteousness*
   *will have control.*

*So cry aloud*
   *from bended knee;*
*a contrite heart weeps,*
   *"Set me free;*

*there is no way*
   *I can escape,*
*my very best's*
   *a ragged cape."*

*"Sweet Lord, I stand*
   *believing You;*
*You did it all*
   *that battle's through.*

*So I shall rest*
   *in faith assured,*
***Your** righteousness*
   *I have secured."*

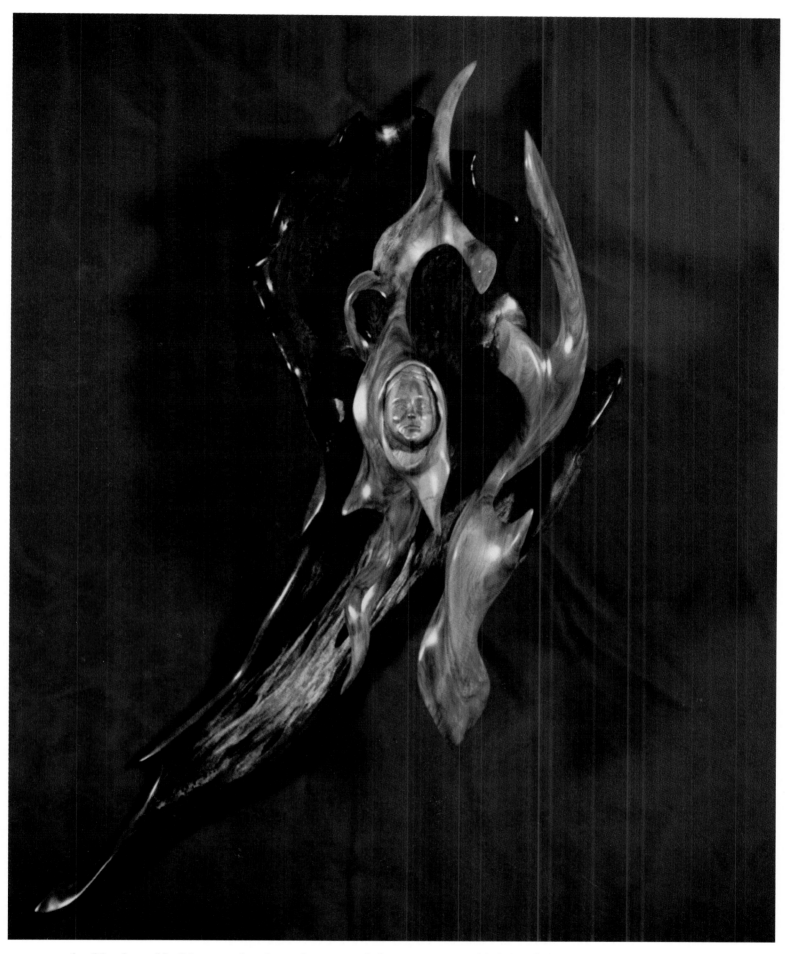

*And be found in him, not having mine own righteousness, which is of the law, but that which is through the faith of Christ, the righteousness which is of God by faith.*
**Philippians 3:9**

West Texas Juniper on Mesquite

Height 14″

# WINDING IT UP

In our formative years we often have things all figured out, until time proves we were anything but accurate. One lazy summer day there was a great gathering of the minds outside on our grade school playground. The problem lay before us, a newly acquired major treasure—a washing machine cardboard box—and no way to utilize it. That day there was an unprecedented number of dust devils (whirlwinds) roaming about over the endless expanses of cotton fields and vacant lots; why, a couple of them had actually come in and tried to carry away our treasure. Often accused of being a quart low on common sense, I made up for it with an overload of speculative genius.

"I've got it! The dust devils are so weakened when they slam into the school building that they are caught off guard and have to shrink. Here is the plan. If we all run against the wind inside one, it will have the same effect and we can shrink it so small that we can clamp the box down over it and we will have our own dust devil captured in a box. It might be something akin to a jinni in a bottle, who knows?"

There is an air of excitement created by being bowled over by a washing machine box and having your face packed with sand. Who can describe the wonder of seeing the box carried high over the power lines, along with your cap. These particular whirling dervishes were insidious and not about to be captured. Finally, our plans worked. We trapped a small one up against the gymnasium wall; it was little more than a tiny column of grass and leaves cowering in the corner. Plop, what stealth, we had it. To prevent its escape we leaned our battered, gasping bodies against the dust devil's prison. "Aladin eat your heart out." After much deliberation, we finally lifted one corner of the box. Dirt-caked eyes bent low to see our prize. Nothing! There was nothing there. Reaching around in the box my hands came back empty. "Oh well, one more day of youth successfully wasted, that is life. On to bigger and better things."

Some twenty years later I found myself repeating those words. I finally had captured my dream of independence and the total control of my destiny. It was a lifetime, not a day, spent in chasing the wind, and there were no bigger and better things on to which to go—only the vivid realization that my precious prize and the treasure of talents God had given me to capture it were as empty as that box of long ago. As King Solomon put it after he had stared into his aging, empty hands, *"Vanity of vanities . . . all is vanity"* (Ecclesiates 1:2). All is striving after the wind.

You know, the end of the road is a great place to turn around and start back toward the God who made you; but, *"blessed are they that have not seen, and yet have believed"* (John 20:29). God would rather we stop in our tracks today and do an about face. The broad road will soil and scar you, and the final step on that road is death. *"To day, if ye will hear his voice, harden not your hearts . . ."* (Hebrews 3:7-8)

When your box of treasures is opened up on judgment day and all your valuables poured out in that glorious light before the throne of God, what will you have? Your material wealth will be back on earth along with your grave; your fame and accomplishments will not make the journey either. *"For what shall it profit a man, if he shall gain the whole world, and lose his own soul? Or what shall a man give in exchange for his soul?"* (Mark 8:36-37) Those are the words of the judge you will be standing before on that day and I believe you know the answer to His question as well. What is valuable to you? The Pearl of great price or something He has created? The judge goes on to say in Mark 8:38, *"Whosoever **therefore** shall be ashamed of me and of my words in this adulterous and sinful generation; of him* [or her] *also shall the Son of man be ashamed, when he cometh in the glory of his Father with the holy angels."* You may say, "Wait a minute. Where did we get off talking about hell, fire and damnation? We were talking about kids and their foolish escapades." Well, we still are. Nothing could be more foolish than loving this present world to the destruction of your own soul. James writes, *"Ye adulterers and adulteresses, know ye not that the friendship of the world is enmity with God? Whosoever therefore will be a friend of the world is the enemy of God"* (James 4:4). There is no middle ground, none. Life is serious business. We may think we have things all figured out and then find out that the very foundations of our values are totally amiss.

The day I saw that the sum total of my abilities and efforts was a big zero, I began an honest approach to God **on my knees.** I came to my Creator, empty handed for I had *repented*, dumped everything I had held onto as good and bad, right and wrong, true and false. I let it go in exchange for His word on the subject of life and death. I bowed my knee and threw myself upon His mercy, believing Him to be a God who is able to justify the ungodly. The only thing truly valuable other than God Himself is to be acceptable in His sight, and that is only possible through *His* efforts not ours.

I have a relationship with Jesus. I value Him above all else. I am not ashamed of Him or the gospel that leads others to know Him, *"for it is the power of God unto salvation to every one who believeth"* (Romans 1:16). I have peace with God—true treasure.

As I write this, I believe I understand what motivated Paul to write: *"Woe is unto me, if I do not preach the gospel!"* (I Corinthians 9:16) Anything else is pointless existence, striving after the wind.

Do not merely take my word for anything in this book. Approach God on your knees. Ask Him to verify or nullify any of these words in the light of His Word. Let go of your rights; repent and believe in Jesus Christ, God's only Son. Trust him as your Lord and Savior.

I thank you for listening, I really do; and I leave you with this one last thought and poem.

Christians, if you really want to realize Jesus at your side, you may have to go join Him in the harvest field.

*When I look into Your heart, Dear Lord,*
*    what more is there to say*
*than there is no doubt You've made us all*
*    and give commands today.*

*And who's to ask what right You have,*
*    and only fools say "no"*
*when the aching heart of the most High God*
*    tells His people, "Rise and go."*

*So when I count the cost so dear*
*    don't let me fail to weigh*
*the dreadful price of choosing death*
*    by going my own way.*

*But I'm so blind, my eyes set on*
*    the things that I let go,*
*not on the prize of knowing You,*
*    the One who loves me so.*

*So I'm on my way, You know my heart,*
*    what's that I hear You say?*
*I'm not going anywhere;*
*    **we** are setting out today.*